DISCIPLESHIP

"A Vital Aspect of Christian Living"

Hollis L. Green, ThD, PhD

GlobalEdAdvancePress
37321-7635 USA

**Dedicated to the memory of a
True Disciple of Jesus Christ who used
Ministry skills to make disciples:**

The Reverend Henry M. Parks, B.D.

~

Discipleship
A Vital Aspect of Christian Living

Copyright © 2007
Global Educational Advance Inc.
Tennessee 37321-7635

Printed in the United States of America
ISBN 978-0-9796019-5-8

First Edition of this book was published by
PATHWAY PRESS 1962
Revised Edition Published by

GlobalEdAdvancePress
37321-7635 USA

Table of Contents

Author's Preface

Modern Man has changed the term "Christian" to meet lower personal standards of various sectarian groups. In many circles, the term no longer means a true believer in Jesus Christ: one who has forsaken all, denied self, taken up the Cross, and is daily following Jesus Christ. One must return to the original term which described the early followers of Christ to properly define the Christian experience. This book brings the terms "disciple" and "Christian" together because it is believed that an understanding of Christian discipleship will give a proper perspective to the whole of Christian living.

A declaration that Jesus Christ has all power prefaced the Great Commission, and it was climaxed by the promise that Christ would always be with His people. The strength of the early church came when they discovered that life is a cooperative venture with God. This changed the disciples into Christ-like men, who became a powerful force for truth in the world. With one voice they proclaimed Christ's death, burial, and resurrection; in "one accord" they witnessed to His living presence. All divisions vanished, and they went forth to bear witness in the power of unity. With this clearly in mind, believers, today, must go forth living the word in every aspect of life. Then it is easy to sacrifice; then it is easy to serve; then it is easy to live and to walk the way of Christian discipleship, because discipleship is a vital aspect of Christian living. This book was originally written in 1962 as a Church Training Course for workers in Christian Education. It is presented again because the need for Discipleship remains. Only a few changes from the original text were made for this edition to make it more gender neutral. The reader is reminded that the "masculine gender bias" that existed in the 1962 edition could not be readily changed. Times have changed and readers expect things to be gender neutral; however, the Bible has not changed and the quotations are from the KJV which remains somewhat masculine. The present task of the author is to write new books, but a few out of print books are being sold on the web at high prices. This reissued edition is to keep the content in the existent literature and bring the book at a reasonable price to new readers. After all, the basic concept of scriptural-based discipleship has not changed, but there are fewer active Christian disciples in the local churches of the 21st Century. Perhaps this scriptural-based text will shed new light on the old message of Christian discipleship as an adventure in living.

Author's Note

A digital CD of this book is available through Post-Gutenberg Books. The author hopes the CD will expedite searching the text for subjects that interest you, and assist with finding the information you want You may give feedback about the Post-Gutenberg Books process of providing searchable digital texts w/voice on CD at: PostGutenbergBks@aol.com.

DAWN OF A NEW DISCIPLINE

Since the flaming sword barred the gate of Eden, Man has traveled a maze of pathways in search of the tree of life. The human family had long awaited a "Messiah Man." The centuries of sin, after the fall, had multiplied the evils of the human race, and all efforts at self-improvement had failed. Providence provided a solution to this human dilemma—Jesus Christ—the Way to God!

God had prepared a time for Jesus to be born. Israel had been prepared by prophecy and promise to be the cradle of a new faith. Judaism was a decaying religion, but it still possessed faith in one God, the highest standard of ethics and family life, and an expectation of a redemptive Messiah. Furthermore, the road system designed for marching Roman legions could be used for missionary pioneers of the new faith, and the Roman peace would, for a season, protect the first disciples of Jesus Christ during the early expansion of Christianity. The time for Christ had come.

Look again at the times: they were full of trouble and despair for Israel and the world system. The Roman peace was kept by a ruthless military dictatorship conjoined with a corrupt religious system. The seeds of Roman destruction; however, had already been planted by the persecuting of Jews, and it would soon turn its fury loose on converts of the new faith. The world seemed destitute of truth and buried in the gross darkness of the times.

I. DEGREES OF DARKNESS

The new discipline to be declared by Jesus Christ did not begin in a religious vacuum. The men of the world were not found wanting for something to believe. The new faith would have to fight against entrenched religious attitudes which had existed for centuries. Most of the religious thinking had degenerated into feeble superstitions and meaningless rituals; others seemed to be new and vigorous.

Despair of Pagan Society

The moral decadence, revealed by the writers of this period, was unbelievable. The religious beliefs of pagan society bred superstition and fear. Most of the world lived in the shadow of death. The light was as darkness and the corrupting forces of evil worked beneath the surface of world order.

Animism. A primitive religion of Man was animism which was based on fear. The belief seemed to be that everything that existed was a god and that the sum total of these gods was the true god. Each family had its own gods. The farmer worshiped the gods of his own farm and fireside. These individual gods personified the forces and the daily hardships with which the individual had to deal in living. The cities of the Roman Empire had their own deities and religious festivities, but the cities soon declined and the people abandoned faith in gods that were unable to aid them against outside forces.

State and Emperor Worship. The Roman conquest had caused decline in the worship of various individual and city deities and gradually there was an increased ascription of superhuman honors to individuals. The growing power of the state and its rulers on the lives of men paved the way for a new type of religion, the worship of the state and the emperor. In this approach to religion, the ruler of the state represented "god" and the subjects were compelled to worship the ruler. Refusal of Christians to participate in such worship later precipitated violent persecution, because Christians have always objected to worshiping a human being or any other creature.

Mystery and Magic. The state religion and emperor worship did not prove satisfying to the people, because it was a collective effort and could not be individually maintained. There was no fellowship with deity and no personal comfort or strength for troubled times offered to the individual. Men seemed to be seeking a more personal faith that would bring them into immediate contact with deity, and they were ready for any sort of experience that would promise them contact with a divine force.

Mysticism. The times gave rise to mysticism. This was

a sign of the world-weariness and deep religious need that marked the decay of the Roman Empire. Mysticism offered an outlet for emotion and satisfied the desire for personal experience and social equality. Mysticism had ritual, formulas, symbols, and secret brotherhoods where all met on a common level. These mysterious religions were emphatically personal, but utterly failed to meet basic human needs and further complicated Man's approach to the true God.

Occultism. Similar to the mystic religions was occultism which enveloped forms of magic and superstitious observance that ensnared the people of pagan societies. The practitioners of such magic believed the entire world to be inhabited by spirits and demons that could be commanded to do one's bidding if only the correct magic rite or formula were used. Foretelling the future through various superstitions, the work of sorcerers and the mania for horoscopes reached a peak during the force of these magic religions.

Darkness of Human Philosophy
Not one religion had solved the problems or answered the questions about Man and God. The search for these answers continued. The false religions of pagan society gave men no hope. Thoughtful men abandoned such religious systems altogether and began to search for a new way to explain themselves and the universe. The empty ritualism and ignorant superstition of false religions had not only complicated basic human religious nature, but caused some to deny that such a nature existed. Thinking men began an attempt to correlate all existing knowledge

about the universe into systematic forms and to integrate human experience with this knowledge. The hope was to attain full comprehension of the mysteries related to human participation with the divine.

To achieve this end, various systems of philosophy were created: Platonism, Gnosticism, Neo-Platonism, Stoicism, Epicureanism, Cynicism, and Skepticism. Some dealt with abstract concepts of the world; others promised salvation by knowledge. New systems of thought appeared which were based on a portion of a preceding philosophy. Certain philosophies could find neither purpose nor design in a world of chance, and these advocated "pleasure" as the highest possible good. Some supplied a philosophic justification for doing what most people did anyway. Some thinkers taught that the world was controlled by an Absolute Reason and that conformity was the highest good. Self-control was the goal of others. Some abandoned all standards and convictions and became complete individualists in an effort to demonstrate individual difference. Some dealt with ethics; others with intellect. None, however, arrived at the truth that God is the ultimate standard by which Man must measure human attitudes and actions.

Human philosophy left the human race destitute of moral and spiritual purpose. The grand truth of monotheism (one God) was obscured as Man grasped in despair for manmade straw gods. The world by its own wisdom could not know the true God. Man could not search out His ways. And even when human reason did glimpse the truth of one living God, he could not determine avenues of worship or what relations God desired to maintain with mankind. Human beings best were far enough from truth to be in gross error. Mankind was still without God and needed redemption.

Dim Twilight of Judaism

Redemption was to come through Israel, but the remaining light of Judaism was twilight of the evening; not of the morning. The Israelite nation had grown old and its vital spirituality had changed into a lifeless formalism. Israel was a weak nation and had lost political independence to mighty Rome. Yet the embers of Messianic hope survived the never-ending succession of catastrophes.

Judaism's God was different from the gods of the religions of the Roman Empire, and faith in this God was the sustaining power. Judaism was free from the worst excesses of the pagan world, but it knew little of a pure and spiritual devotion, or acceptable spiritual service to God. Israel was strangely backward in the philosophy and science of the day, but compared with other people, the Jews stood in the "twilight of truth." The Old Testament terminates with words of hope and promise: "The Lord, whom ye seek, shall suddenly come..." (Malachi 8:1). Those persons who kept this expectation were not disappointed. The New Testament opens with the news of the divine daybreak - the coming of the Christ child to be the redeeming light of the world.

II. DAWN OF SACRED DUTY

The twilight of Judaism's truth was eclipsed by the darkness of the time, but beneath the despair of the people was the slumbering force of an indestructible hope. Israel looked toward the night but hoped for the bright and morning star. The birth of Jesus was the divine daybreak that was to bring the dawn of sacred duty to all men.

Divine Daybreak

The dayspring from on high was to give light to those who sat in darkness and in the shadow of death and to guide their feet in the way of peace (Luke 1:78, 79). The gaze of preceding generations had fixed a hope on the coming Messiah. No generation in human history had needed salvation and peace more that the one in which Jesus was born. An evening of darkness hovered about Bethlehem and the world slept in despair. It was time for the "true Light" to penetrate the night and to point the way to God. The "Sun of righteousness" promised by Malachi was to dispel the darkness, and the divine sunrise was to bring light to the world. The good news was first given to the sleeping shepherds who were in the fields near Bethlehem, but since that glorious daybreak the news has been carried to the uttermost part of the earth.

Dawn of Duty

The angelic pronouncement of the Messiah's advent and the harmony of the heavenly hosts that told of peace on earth and good will among men compelled the shepherds to investigate immediately. The shepherds were among the common folk who hated war and the personal strife caused by the sins of Man and who longed for personal peace with God and true peace among their fellow men. The birth of the Messiah would change all this. Note the sequence of the actions of the shepherds: without delay they searched for and worshiped the Christ child; made known the angelic message; caused others to marvel at the wonderful news; returned to their routine tasks glorifying and praising God that they were a part of such an occasion. (Luke 2:8-18). The angelic host and the personal magnetism of Jesus had transformed the sleeping shepherds into shouting men. They had been trusted with a heavenly message, and the shepherds had told it well. Thus, the common person had been awakened to a sacred human duty –seek and worship Christ the Redeemer!

For many years wise men searched the limits of human knowledge, probing the unlimited reaches of the heavens for a sign to guide in their worship of a true God. With the first glimpse of the Star of Bethlehem came the dawn of sacred duty to the wise men, and they were constrained by "His Star" to search for and worship the newborn King.

Daylight of a Life

The first cry of the Christ-child was evidence that God had sent into the world a life that would be "the light of men." As the angelic proclamation had pointed the shepherds to the Savior and as the star guided the wise men to Bethlehem, the life and redemptive activity of Jesus Christ was to direct men to God. His life was a life of quality. It was a sinless life nurtured in Nazareth, a most unlikely place for holy development, but Jesus grew in wisdom, stature, and in favor with God and Man. It was the custom of Jesus to attend the synagogue regularly and to be taught the discipline of Judaism. (Luke 4:16). Jesus shared with other Jewish boys the thrill of the ancient Scriptures.

At the age of twelve Jesus became a "son of the law" and visited the Temple in Jerusalem. Already a maturing sense of dedication was evident as the boy Jesus went about to do the heavenly Father's business with no effort to gain a personal reputation. (Luke 2:46, 47; Philippians 2:7). When God took upon Himself the form of human flesh, it was no longer necessary that mankind be utterly depraved. In the perfect life of Jesus, redemption had appeared.

III. DIVINE DIDACTIC

The years passed in silence after Jesus visited the Temple until the time that He was baptized in Jordan by John to "fulfill all righteousness." Just as Jesus had shared with the human family a body of flesh, a normal family life, and the discipline of growth, now He shares the new hope that is prevalent in Galilee and is baptized to prepare for an active ministry of teaching. Jesus was a true didactic, a teacher of principles, precepts and doctrines to instruct the people in righteousness. Jesus purposely allies Himself with the best of His generation and publicly identifies Himself with the new religious force that demands repentance and righteousness.Jesus made no public claim to deity in His early ministry, but at the wedding in Cana He wrought what John describes as the "beginning of His signs" of Sonship.

Jesus then traveled to Jerusalem and cleansed the Temple of the money-changers and claimed that His future death and resurrection were His authority. Jesus began to teach in the synagogues and to answer questions concerning the meaning and application of the commandments, the correct teachings of the resurrection, and to give judgment in legal matters. (Luke 12:13). This corresponds with the normal work of the Jewish Rabbi (Teacher), who was both theologian and jurist.

Divine Authority

The divine authority of Jesus Christ is the foundation of His teaching. Jesus made pronouncements on matters commonly regarded as carrying divine sanction – the Sabbath, forgiveness, and the Temple. Jesus frequently said, "Verily, verily, I say unto you..." echoing the divine "amen" of ancient days. Jesus proclaimed with directness and authority the nearness of the Kingdom and called for immediate decision on the part of the listeners. Jesus repeatedly challenged the sacred Torah by saying "Ye have heard that it hath been said by them of old time... but I say unto you....!"

The Torah is the first division of the Hebrew canon and contains the five books of the Law. In addition to the written Torah, the Pharisees and rabbis recognized an oral Torah (law) which comprised specific applications of the principles of the written law. Oral traditions had become as minute and devoid of spiritual meaning as to set aside the Law of God (Matthew 15:2; Mark 7:9, 18; Colossians 2:8).

Although Jesus was a Jew, He was loyal to Judaism only when Judaism was faithful to the truth. Jesus never confused truth and tradition and placed loyalty to the Father before devotion to Judaism. Jesus did not challenge the authority of the written law, but supplemented it with additional divine utterance making it more demanding. The authority of Jesus was evidenced by His refusal to argue or to debate. He simply declared the truth of His discipline and the truth stood for itself. This is authority!

The authority of Jesus differed profoundly from that of the Jewish Rabbis. A rabbi was an interpreter of Scripture who always spoke from derived authority. The teaching of Jesus was never merely interpretation of a given sacred text; he used the Law and quoted or referred to sacred Scripture at least four hundred times in teaching the people who followed Him. Jesus spoke from personal authority. There was nothing in contemporary Judaism that corresponded to the immediacy with which Jesus taught. The authority of God and the reality of divine will were always directly present and fulfilled in Jesus Christ.

Jesus was different from the other teachers of the day. Every fact reveals this distinction. There was an active freshness about His teaching. Jesus taught in the synagogues and traveled as an itinerant along the roads of Palestine, but others had taught in the open and used some of the same methods. The difference was the man and His message. The uniqueness of Jesus is clearly seen in what He taught and in who He was. A strange crowd pressed upon Him everywhere He traveled: in open fields, by a sea shore, or atop a hill the common people gathered in multitudes to hear His words of wisdom. Farmers and fishermen were taught by Jesus; little children felt at ease in His presence; sinners who heard Jesus found forgiveness and a new hope. Even the officials of Judaism who heard Him said, "Never a man spoke like this man."

In the course of His teaching, Jesus healed the sick, forgave sins, fed the hungry, and calmed the elements of nature. His teaching and conduct made Him a person of distinction, a teacher different from anyone the people had seen or heard.

Demonstration of Deity

Jesus demonstrated His deity in numerous ways. In addition to the voice of divine authority, Jesus healed the sick, worked miracles, and forgave sins. The people knew He was different, but the opinions of the people concerning Him were divided. Some thought because of his miraculous power that Jesus was John the Baptist raised from the dead (John 7:40-43). His prophetic authority caused some to think He was Elijah. A few even thought Jesus was Jeremiah because of his tenderness. The people knew Jesus was no ordinary prophet, but they did not clearly grasp the truth of His deity.

Jesus had not claimed to be the Messiah because the term could easily be misunderstood. Even when John had sent Jesus a perplexed inquiry from prison asking if He were the Messiah, Jesus answered with a description of the things that were taking place in His ministry. The disciples of John were instructed by Jesus to tell John: "The blind receive their sight and the lame walk, the lepers are cleansed, and the deaf hear, the dead are raised up, and the poor have the gospel preached to them" (Matthew 11:3-5).

Jesus chose to demonstrate His deity and to impress upon each individual the fact that He was the Son of

God.   In some instances Jesus waited for the truth of His deity to break its own light upon the heart. On one occasion in Jerusalem a number of Jews gathered about Him in the Temple and asked: "How long dost thou make us to doubt? If thou be the Christ, tell us plainly." Jesus answered: "The works that I do in my Father's name, they bear witness of me" (John 10:24, 25).   When the light of this truth finally broke into the inner circle of His disciples, Jesus had reached the point toward which He had worked for nearly three years. It was revealed to Simon Peter that Jesus was "the Christ, the Son of the living God." With the Twelve convinced of His Sonship, Jesus could proceed on the course that would lead to Calvary.

IV. DISCIPLINE DECLARED

Looking at the tragic need of the world, Jesus had a formidable task: changing mankind's course to the direction of righteousness. Yet Jesus did not hesitate to put Himself to God's redemptive work. The first step was to set in motion efforts to build new men for a new society through discipline.

Discipline Defined

Discipline is defined as the system of rules affecting conduct or action, and it implies instruction and correction, the training which improves, molds, strengthens, and perfects character. It is the moral education obtained by the enforcement of obedience through supervision and control. The purpose of moral discipline is the correction, the improvement, the obedience, the faith, and the faithfulness of disciples.

The discipline of Jesus was addressed to the inner person—what an individual should be in desire and in thought. Jesus recognized the acts of individuals as expressions of an inner life and thought accordingly.   He was more interested in people than precepts. The truth is that the new discipline was qualitatively a new and a different attitude – a predisposition to act in a particular manner. Jesus avoided rigid concepts that could not be universally applied, and He placed in the mind and soul the true seeds of spiritual thought that would grow and flower with faith, maturity, and experience. Jesus taught principles rather than specific rules that gave the discipline of Jesus validity and permanency and confined His teaching to eternal values devoid of the legalistic Judaism characteristic of the period.

The eyes of Jesus penetrated the life of a person and saw them exactly as they were. With no reservation, Jesus described people frankly and sincerely. Note the procession of unlovely people that paraded through His teachings, each clearly exposed because of divine discernment: a rude neighbor refuses bread, an unwise farmer had no thought of the future, a high-living glutton ignores the beggar, an impatient youth deserts home; a judge rules unjustly, a steward juggles his books, a lazy servant buries his talent, a heartless banker forecloses on a widow's mortgage, and an envious farmer sows tares in a neighbor's crop. This was a tough crowd to teach moral and ethical living.

A positive aspect in the discipline of Jesus was lacking in other religious teachings. Two basic characteristics contributed to the inspirational power and effectiveness of

His discipline: First, the discipline of Jesus had a spiritual basis, deriving its imperative from the divine nature and will. It had a divine goal—to make trust in God the root and principle of all goodness and to make individuals in the image of Christ. Second, the discipline of Jesus was exemplified in His own life. Jesus taught as effectively by example as He did by precept. Discipleship or following Christ came to mean not only the acceptance of certain principles of right and compliance with certain demands, but a supreme loyalty to a Person in whom these principles had received concrete embodiment and fulfillment. There is no parallel to the personal influence of Jesus Christ in the lives of believers.

Jesus defined the essential quality of a moral act by teaching the principle of love and the law of right conduct (Luke 10:27; Mark 12:28-31). The concept of right conduct presupposes the law of love and is distinctive from this love. The law of love produces right conduct. It is the motive alone which gives moral quality to action. This absolute inwardness of moral law is the underlying theme of the teachings of Jesus. With Jesus, the heart was the seat of all virtue and the spring of all truly righteous conduct (Luke 19:27; Mark 12:28-31).

The exceptional way Jesus proclaimed His view had momentous consequences both negative and positive. Jesus broke with Judaism and His own people by rejecting ceremonialism and legalism and by declaring a positive and an active spiritual force which is divinely imparted to the heart. These factors led to a profound emphasis on moral purity and on a lofty moral ideal. It was this fact that transformed human love into holy love and gave the Christian doctrine of love a spiritual comprehensiveness.

Development of the Disciple

The quality of simplicity distinguished the disciples of Jesus. The basic appeal of His teaching is always in an innate knowledge of the truth, to the inner discernment, the moral sense of ordinary folk. Jesus talked of the heavenly Father who loves and reigns. He discoursed on life within the Father's family, of brotherliness, sympathy, forgiveness, and love. Jesus opened up endless possibilities of the power of prayer and the victories of faith. Whatever problems His words may raise, of faith or more often of obedience, we rarely are in doubt of what Jesus meant. The difficulties are not in understanding but in doing.

The methods used to advance the development of spiritual discipline often caused listeners to admit the truth being taught or provoked the recognition of truth by the listener's own thought processes. Jesus was effective in the use of short pointed statements to stimulate basic understanding of His discipline. He posed innumerable questions to relate outward conduct to inward character. In the course of teaching, Jesus used dramatic conversions to teach that He was the forgiver.

Jesus had a dramatic force in His manner of telling a story to illustrate the truth that He taught, and He used an exceptional economy of words. The parables which Jesus told contained hidden truths. He used this simple method to explain eternal truths and was usually easily understood by the average listener, because He took the stories from everyday circumstances. No summary is adequate to do justice to the wealth of meaning contained in the parables Jesus used to teach the people simple truths. Seeing all His parables as a whole, their method becomes illuminated and the message is crystallized. If one understands the parables of Jesus, the basic message to mankind becomes clear: love God and enjoy His blessings forever.

The essential elements of character expected by Jesus are expressed in the Beatitudes (Matthew 5:3-11). Those who were brought under the new discipline must be bankrupt in spirit and utterly dependent on God, penitent of sin and willing to share the burdens of others, be Christ-controlled and ready to obey, earnestly desirous of the righteousness of God; merciful, truly righteous with no mixed motives, a peacemaker and able to joy in suffering and persevere during persecution. This then is a true disciple!

The character produced by the new discipline was to result in spiritual influence. This is the divine intention of Jesus. Those who live in the attitude of the Beatitudes will realize a threefold law of influence: **Salt** - that preserves and prevents corruption. **Light** - that points the way and **City** - the realization of social order and progress. Then Jesus adds that these disciples will be a light shining before men because of their good works and will influence others to follow their example and glorify the heavenly Father (Matthew 5:13-16).

Demands of the Discipline

The strongly worded principles of Jesus in the Sermon on the Mount have served as a practical guide to turn minds and hearts more strongly to His teaching and have incorporated the spirit of the constructs in daily activities. Several basic characteristics and demands of the righteousness required are prominent:

Jesus demanded an exceeding righteousness.

A firm requirement of the new discipline was a new righteousness that exceeds that of the Scribes and Pharisees (Matthew 5:20).   Jesus declared that the Kingdom's righteousness was superior to that practiced by the most learned Scribes and the most zealous Pharisees in the Jewish community. Jesus affirmed that negative goodness alone was not sufficient to meet the standard of the new discipline. External conformity to the letter of the Law was not enough. Those who would follow Jesus must have their hearts changed, for their inner selves must be consecrated to the cause of truth.

Jesus demanded a righteousness springing out of love.

The new discipline given and lived by Jesus goes beyond Jewish law, but it does not annul it. The demands of the Law and the Prophets are not cancelled; they become flesh and blood and live among men in the persona and work of Jesus Christ. Jesus exemplified the Law in His own life and gave it a higher and richer fulfillment. Jesus took the six hundred and thirteen laws and transformed them into the "Law of Love:" that was extended to include the enemy. The moral dynamics of this love will yet transform the lives of men.

The importance Jesus attached to the demands of His discipline is marked by the abundance of detail with which He illustrated the constructs. The manifesto of the Messiah on moral conduct was clear and compelling. The changes in the discipline of Jesus can be seen in His concentration on essential points of human life and in His re-evaluation of ancient values. In the Sermon on the Mount, Jesus translated the requirements of the Law into the demands of a new discipline (Matthew chapters 5-7).

Jesus demanded more respect for the individual.

The first contrast between the Law and the new discipline was in the requirement dealing with murder. Jesus required dignity for the individual. He condemned murder, but equally condemned anger against one's brother. Jesus stated that contempt or despising of another was in danger of punishment from the highest court and that any personal insult was in danger of hell-fire.

Jesus demanded more honor for womanhood.

Jesus' words on adultery are perhaps the most searching words ever uttered concerning immorality. Jesus declared that even an evil eye offends the heart and makes it guilty of immorality. The Law permitted the breaking of the family relationship by divorce, but Jesus pointedly stated that nothing should soil or in any way pollute marriage, the foundation of the family and the home. He did not say that nothing "could" weaken the foundation of marriage. This was viewed later as an ideal situation and exceptions began to creep into the sacred literature. This together with a progressive decline in social morals has brought the family to the brink of disgrace.

Jesus demanded more esteem for one's reputation.

The old standard permitted an individual to substantiate the truth with the goodness of another by swearing an oath. The new discipline declared that the character of citizens of the Kingdom should be unquestionable, making the oath unnecessary. A simple "yes" and "no" answer would be sufficient for a person who had an honest report.

Jesus demanded more initiative in friendship.

Under the Law the neighbor was to be loved, but the enemy could be hated. Jesus gave love a new basis and an added dimension and said that revenge is to be left to God and that His followers were to love and to pray for their enemies. Jesus required the offended to take the initiative in repairing relationships.

Jesus demanded true motives in worship.

The new discipline required the giving of alms as a silent part of worship to God and not openly for show. The followers of Jesus were to pray with simple faith in secret and were to live a positive life and keep a cheerful countenance even when afflicted with the burden of fasting.

Jesus demanded faith in the future.

The followers of Christ were not to be fearful of the future. Jesus taught that it was unnecessary to lay up earthly treasures that would perish but that one should lay up spiritual treasures in heaven. Material gains were to be used for the advancement of the Kingdom to insure their continued desire to enter into the Kingdom. They were to have one Master and trust Him absolutely for their daily needs, food, shelter, raiment, health, employment. They were to seek the Kingdom first and to trust God with the future.

Jesus demanded honest dealings with others.

Jesus taught that men should be concerned about others, but He warned about passing judgment on them. No individual could have all the facts; therefore, God was the Judge of all. The time should be more wisely spent examining one's own faith. The spiritual needs of others were to be considered, and a spiritual witness was to be given to those willing to listen. Jesus declared that the good things of the Father belonged to His followers, for the asking. Jesus demanded that others be treated as they desired to be treated themselves.

The listeners on the mountain that heard Jesus make the demands of His discipline were told that the test of their character would be in the way they walked: the narrow way or the broad way. They were warned against false teachers and false fruit and told that every believer must bear fruit, and that they would be known by their fruit. Jesus declared that all profession must be practiced to substantiate the new discipline, and that the final test would be the foundation of their spiritual Rock, the house would stand the storms of life. When Jesus had ended His declaration of the new discipline, the people were astonished at His doctrine: "For he taught them as one having authority, and not as the scribes" (Matthew 7:13-29).

Study and Review Questions for Section One

1   What was the condition of the world at the birth of Jesus?

2   What similarity did the ministry of Jesus have with the normal work of the Jewish Rabbi? How was it different?

3   Discuss the divine authority of Jesus.

4   How did Jesus demonstrate His deity?

5   What effect did the teaching of principles rather than specific rules have on the ethical teachings of Jesus?

6   What basic characteristics contributed to the power and effectiveness of the new discipline?

7   Discuss the demands of the new discipline.

DIALOGUE WITH DEITY

Life is essentially dialogue; that is, a conversation between two or more individuals. No one can live or die to himself. It was not good for a man to be alone in Eden, because he was not complete in himself. Relating his life to others would bring a fulfillment of destiny. The most beautiful part of life in Eden was found in Adam's walking in harmony and in complete fellowship with the Creator.

Why did God make humans? Adam was created to keep and to dress the Garden of Eden and to satisfy the yearning of the Father heart of God. From the first inspired record of God walking with Adam in the cool of the Garden to the final vision of the New Jerusalem descending from heaven that God might dwell with us, the underlying message of the Scriptures has been of a God who desires to come forth and meet with Humanity.

V. DIALOGUE—GOD WITH MAN

The first question of the Westminster Catechism reads: "What is the chief end of Man?" The answer: "Man's chief end is to glorify God and to enjoy Him forever." What about the purpose of God in this matter?

The story is told of a little girl which illustrates the true meaning of this answer. It seems that a godly mother, putting her child to bed, had asked the first question in the catechism and had received the proper answer. Then the mother, not quite realizing why, asked: "And darling, what do you think is the chief end of God?" Pondering a moment, the child replied: "If the chief end of Man is to glorify God and enjoy Him forever, then I suppose the chief end of God must be to glorify Man and to enjoy him forever." Out of the mouths of babes come words of wisdom. Not only does logic affirm that the converse of a proposition is also true, the Word of God confirms this to be the divine purpose. God's delight is with His creation. It is clear that fellowship with a redeemed person is dear to the heart of God.

Conversation through Adam

When God made Man in His image, He made an intelligent being with whom He could converse about the beauties of creation. Adam was the keeper of God's garden and God talked with Him. Today, it is difficult to imagine the joy and refreshment of such conversation. Man was not made only to glorify God, but to enjoy God and to be God's joy. Many see only the first part and think that they must wait until after death to begin enjoying God. The conversation between God and Adam assures us that we were made to do both now. Man fulfilled his highest destiny when he communed "naked" before his Creator in the Garden. The heartbreak of God occurred when sin spoiled this holy fellowship.

Covenant through Abraham

After the fall, God begins to separate from the sons of men those who would listen to His voice. He longed for fellowship with mankind. Enoch and Noah were said to have "walked with God," but God was searching for someone who would yield completely to divine will. In Abraham, God found a man to father a family and build a nation. The people of God received a covenant through Abraham—a covenant for ultimate redemption and complete restoration to fellowship with God. The divine plan to bring mankind back to full fellowship was constantly marred by evil, but God set apart the descendants of Abraham as His "peculiar treasure:" a people of His own. The construct of "peculiar" comes to Scripture from the Latin *peculium* meaning exclusive or private property. God's plan was to purify for Himself a people—to be His very own. Through this covenant remnant God produced Jesus Christ.

Communion through Christ

In the Gospels, God comes still nearer to His creation through the Incarnation (John 1:14). The fellowship with mankind is placed on a more intimate basis: God sent His Son to dwell on earth, and in human flesh He partook of human suffering and temptation. The participation of Jesus Christ in the affairs of Humanity and His willingness to share the plight of the human family clearly bear witness of God's desire for communion and fellowship with mankind. Calvary gives this fellowship a new dimension.

At Pentecost again the Divine invades the human. The Book of Acts transports mankind to the present dispensation and finds God nearest of all to the human family, the

Person of the Holy Spirit, taking up His abode in blood-redeemed hearts. Until the ultimate glorification of the body, the indwelling of the Holy Spirit is the satisfying of the Father's heart for spiritual fellowship with His children.

VI. DIALOGUE--MAN WITH GOD

It is through Jesus Christ that people can be restored to proper relationship with God the Father and can live together in the community of the redeemed. Mankind was made in the image of God. To dwell together in proper interpersonal relationship, human beings must be reconciled to God and be conformed to the image of Christ. Redemption and restoration to fellowship with God is a prerequisite to maintaining proper relationship with other people. This is the beauty of the Christian faith—believers in harmony and agreement, because they are in proper relationship with God.

Conversation Restored

The conversation between God and humans was broken abruptly when sin entered the Garden. Any dialogue after that was a painful thing, and as Adam and Eve hid themselves in the Garden to avoid the searching of God, so people today attempt to avoid the searching experience of spiritual conviction. God desired to restore mankind to proper fellowship and to re-establish a mutually enjoyable conversation. The work on the Cross brought about a conversion experience which would change one's life and reconcile the individual to God.

Calvary Encounter. God seeks to secure a personal encounter with individuals—a Calvary encounter. This is entering into a two-way covenant with God of absolute love and devotion, based upon redeeming love revealed in Christ. Sin separated Man from God, but Calvary is the place of reconciliation.

Conversion Experience. God will step into the life of any person who will walk the Calvary road, and this person will experience conversion. This experience takes place when the individual is made aware of personal sinfulness, self-centeredness, and confronts the Incarnate God at Calvary. The will is bowed and redirected toward God in total surrender and fusion with the will of God, and human emotions are stirred by this tremendous experience. The Calvary encounter or conversion is completed when a person, seeking to find realization and fulfillment of one's essential nature, accepts forgiveness of sins and is restored to fellowship with God.

When anyone takes the step by faith toward God that individual is transformed, and can again enjoy the original conversation with God. One must put himself on record as being committed to the will of God which cannot merely be an outward compliance or external submission, but must be a completely and sincerely forsaking of sins and a devoted following of Jesus. However, though the will of God is the turning point in submission, the Son of God is the turning Person. Jesus is the Mediator between God and Humanity.

Companionship with Christ
A genuinely Christian person is living each moment in personal fellowship with God through Jesus Christ.

Converted and identified with Christ, the believer begins to enjoy true companionship with Deity and becomes a partaker or sharer of the divine nature and becomes a joint heir with Jesus. The personal encounter of the believer continues to be a searching experience in the life of every Christian. Jesus Christ becomes the believer's living contemporary to share constantly life's daily problems.

God calls disciples to absolute conformity to the image of Christ. Nothing less than this did God propose and with nothing less should the believer be content. God called believers to fellowship with His Son on earth, both in His sufferings and His joys. The object of God's call is that Humanity might be holy now and have full fellowship with God. As a person draws nearer to God the Father, he is conscious of the divine presence and companionship with the risen Lord. The believer's countenance radiates the glow of God's glory and personal faith gives substance to the presence of Christ until the words of his prayers, by faith, are as satisfying as if the Master's garment had been touched. This is the personal closeness God desires with believers.

VII. DIALOGUE—MAN WITH MAN

A person who has never been redeemed and restored to fellowship with God has been deprived of full personality development and is constantly in difficulty with others. However, when individuals are converted they come to know each other as new creatures in Christ, and have taken the first step toward developing satisfying human relations. When Christ becomes the center of a life, and divine love becomes the life force, no disturbance can alter this living relationship.

Circle of Human Experience

From the Christian point of view, the center of all things is divine love. With this in mind, let us look at the full circle of human experience and relationship.

The First Half-Circle. The starting point of the first half-circle of ones experience is the individual. A person either thinks of self or of others and the attitude is determined by a mature relationship with God. In this part of the circle of human relationships, individuals usually use others for personal advantage. There is little or no regard for the privileges and rights of others when they distract from personal desires. The "we" of joint activity may only be the enlargement of the "I" and not really mean anything. A corporate task may be credited to the leader with no mention of those who actually made the accomplishment. In this half-circle, everything seems to focus on the individual.

The Second Half-Circle. In the second half-circle of human experience individuals relate to others. The essence of being is not in the individual. This can be found only when individuals are associated with others in the unity of person to person. Proper relationship with other persons is basic to the whole circle of human experience and activity. Man is essentially man with man and life is continued involvement with others in mutually related tasks. When a person is restored to fellowship with God, that person cannot live in complete loneliness and solitude.   The experience can not long remain a solitary thing. One must become concerned with others. The Christian must build a satisfying relationship with everyone.

Christian Concept of Humanity

This begs the ultimate question: What is the Christian concept of Humanity (Man/Mankind/Humankind)? One school of thought tries to understand human beings as they relate to the rest of the world. When this idea is accepted, humans lose value and meaning and become just another part of the world of "things." The proper attitude is illustrated by those who would interpret the world in terms of Humanity. This group believes that God made the beauties of earth and then placed humans there to enjoy both the Creator and the creation. This question cannot be completely answered without considering the one perfect man, Jesus Christ. For the Christian, the point of decision is the revelation of the manifestation of the true and perfect man in Jesus Christ.   Humankind, the creation of God, was corrupted by sin and separated from divine fellowship; however, through Jesus Christ, a person can be reconciled to God and be restored to full fellowship.

Christian Harmony in Human Relations

The will of God brings people into contact with others. Believers must be certain that this contact measures up to Christian standards. Living in harmony with others, assisting them, being a Christian example, and cooperating with them for the common good is the Christian minimum. A joint believer encounter, as radii of a circle, forms the spokes of "togetherness" with Christ as its center. Here individuals can dwell in love, worship God, and participate in Christian activity. This happens when people are willing to commit themselves to Christ and to take their stand together for Christian conduct.

Christian Triangle Encounter. The triangular relationship among Christians is insisted upon in the Scriptures. The person who loves God must love others, even an enemy. The closer one gets to God the more intimate and more harmonious their relationship becomes with others. The converse is true: when one drifts from God there is considerable deterioration in human relationships (See Figure 1, 2, and 3). The language of prayer Jesus taught His disciples gives evidence of a collective concern for the group. Jesus taught them to pray "**Our** Father...Give **us**... forgive **us**...as **we** forgive...lead **us**...deliver **us**...."   The plural is obvious. When an individual is in full fellowship with God, they have a burning desire to live peaceably with all others. The problem of the unredeemed is that no amount of "human engineering" can simulate the spiritual fellowship of believers.

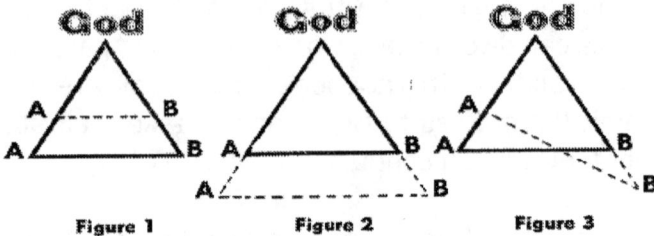

Figure 1   Figure 2   Figure 3

TRIANGLE RELATIONSHIP. The relationship between A and B illustrated here is in direct relation to
their relationship with God. Figure 1 shows that as A and
B get closer to God they are closer to one another. Figure
2 illustrates the strain in human relations when both A
and B drift away from God. Figure 3 shows the change
that takes place when A draws closer to God and B
drifts away. This situation often complicates both the
spiritual life and the human relations of A and B.

There can be no Christian fellowship until individuals
have first shared a common relationship with Christ. It
must be a triangular encounter—a three-way relationship.
Human beings may associate with one another in daily
living, but they will never really know and understand one
another until they meet together in the presence of God.
Christian love leaves no room for the usual bitterness
that plagues and weakens human relations. A life of love
causes one to see the connection between God and Man
and demonstrates the real meaning of one's life in Christ.
It is evident that the more one knows of Christ and His
love, the more love he will have both for Christ and for his
fellowman.

Fellowship with God is the key to proper human relations.
This is the subject of the First Epistle of John. John declared
that the basis of spiritual fellowship was fellowship with the
Father through a union with Jesus Christ. Believers who
live and walk in the true Light of God will have fellowship

with God, and once this fellowship is established one can be assured of a satisfying relationship with others. Without fellowship with God, human relations cannot be essentially right.

Harmony in human relations often depends on what one is making of their personal life. The structure of life must be built upon the Word of God; however, inter-personal relations depend on (1) the climate of one's personality, (2) the standards by which others are measured, and (3) the basic motives that determine one's acts. The Christian experience meets the needs in each of these areas. When people join together in an effort to build their lives after God's plan, they are bound to get along with each other.

A wrong relationship with God is the root of all unchristian conduct. God desires that men live together in the "realm of redemption." Sin in the life of an individual causes his relationship with God to be changed, and his relationship with others disturbed. Likewise any disturbance in the personal relations of two believers hinders their spiritual fellowship with God (First Peter 3:7). It is a three-way interaction, a triangular relationship or nothing.

People often think that they are having trouble with their fellowman, when actually they themselves are out of touch with God and are in trouble spiritually. These differences often lead to the "futile fuss of talk." It should be remembered that a sinner is the victim of human nature and quarrels because of that nature. It takes the work of divine authority to correct this, but it can be done through simple faith in God. God can change the diverse fractions of human behavior into the common denominator of His grace through Jesus Christ. Transformed by the power of His Cross, the will of God becomes clearly seen, human barriers melt away, and men with varying personalities can bow together in worship and in love. It is in Jesus Christ that people get together; He is the one access route for all men to the Father. When individuals sincerely pray about differences, they will discover that the positive virtues flowing out of their Christian love causes a joining of forces to do God's will.

When individuals are transformed by God's redemptive love and are gathered into a Christian community, they are eager to cooperate for edification and evangelism. As the Spirit weaves the scarlet thread of redemptive benefits into the pattern of interpersonal relations, believers grow in spiritual companionship and in concern for others.

Companionship with Christians. A dynamic, growing, transforming spiritual experience compels individuals into wholesome companionship with other believers. Redeemed individuals work together in group life and activity, but always remain an individual on a personal basis with God. Walking with other believers in Christian fellowship is a searching experience. The believer accepts this new companionship as new creatures in Christ, and forgiven sins are forgotten. While there remains a clear distinction between persons, yet believers set apart from the world assume a common identity and bond of peace in the Spirit. Fellowship that is Christian sanctifies all of life and creates a oneness among believers. This God-created unity is not meant to make believers into unhappy satellite souls burdened by the monotony of similarity, but it is concerned with the believers' common devotion to Christ, mutual fellowship, and beneficial united action for Christ.

The spiritual life of believers could not long remain a solitary thing. They must not only have a relationship with God, but they must have fellowship with other Christians. The Christian experience becomes void if it is deprived of fellowship with other believers. Should Christians discover one another in an un-churched community, they should not think of the church as being "back home," but they should unite to function as a vital part of the living church. Saints experience great joy when they unite and then watch the emerging church grow, especially when this growth is out of their having gathered together in Christ.

Christians dwelling together in fellowship form a spiritual community that demonstrates the love of Christ. Since love must first be learned by experiencing love, God teaches us to love by first loving Him. "He that loveth is born of God and knoweth God." The Christian finds a basic need for inter-personal love and companionship met by the divine love and Christian fellowship. Because of God's indwelling love, Christians love one another with fervency and a purity unattainable by any other group on earth.

There is a creativeness in Christian companionship. God ministers His own strength to a believer by sending assistance through a fellow Christian. The primary concern of God's plan for perfecting the saints is to make the individual in the image of Christ. When Christians assist one another in spiritual growth, they share with God the effort to make individuals in the image and likeness of Christ.

Christians have a right to expect consensus in the joint activity. Sincere Christians will be agreeable and respectable to one another even when they disagree. In other words they can disagree agreeably. They should move through a problem-solving experience with assurance that God is pointing the way. When the solution is found, they should say "This seemed good to the Spirit and to us." Observing how Christians meet the problems of life should be an evangelizing, convicting experience to sinners.

Christ's Ambassador to the Unconverted. Believers united for common action must have Christ's redeeming concern and must relay His love to the unconverted. Evangelism is not optional service for a genuine Christian. Believers speak of spiritual things with joy and with an easy naturalness. There is no pious display or morbid fear; the believer's personality diffuses the fragrance of Christ's love and saving grace.

Everyone searches for a person or cause worthy of their energies and loyalties. The Christian cause offers the only adequate Person or cause for complete commitment. Each believer is to be an ambassador for Christ and represent His saving grace among men. Christians are sent as Christ was sent—to plead with human beings. The true believer will have a sense of evangelistic mission in all that is done. Such believers will feel constrained to perform one's personal sacred duty.

Study and Review Questions for Section Two

1. What is the chief end of Man(Mankind, Humankind)?
2. How is Humanity restored to fellowship with God? How does this effect one's relationship with others?
3. Why is the second half circle of human experience important to the Christian?
4. What is the Christian concept of Humanity?
5. Discuss the triangle relationship.

DYNAMICS OF DISCIPLESHIP

A fundamental fact in human conduct is that every action must be motivated by some factor. This is true not only in the physical realm, but it is true even more so in the spiritual area. A spiritual nature is the human's chief possession, and when this nature is stimulated to constructive conduct one is motivated by a master passion. Jesus Christ is the motivation behind Christian discipleship. Jesus is the dynamic force that becomes the disciple's Master power.

The general picture evoked by the Gospels is one of a strong movement stirred up by Jesus among the people. Crowds pressed around Him, listened eagerly to His words, and were amazed at the authority of His teachings. They sought His healing power and praised the miracles He performed. As a result of His ministry, many persons attached themselves to Jesus in varying degrees of conviction and loyalty. This frames the many individual scenes from the story of Jesus, but these followers do not constitute His disciples. To follow someone from place to place does not mean discipleship.

VIII. DISCIPLESHIP DEFINED

The disciple is a pupil or a learnerthatcomes under the discipline and influence of another. The disciple learns certain principles from the teacher and maintains them on the teacher's authority. The term involves a combination of ideas of learning and of serving and even leaves room for elements of immaturity and imperfection. It is a term appropriately related to God's original idea of creating Man in His own image and in His likeness. Man was created in God's image in the sense that he could share God's interest, commune with Him, and share His work in the world. Man was not like God, infinite in knowledge and in understanding, or in any other divided attributes. Rather, was endowed with the capacity to learn from God and to be instructed or disciplined by divine authority.

A broad and a narrow use of the term is discernible in the Gospels and is seen to the best advantage in connection with the choice of the *twelve disciples.* This group of disciples *par excellence* was chosen from a large company of disciples. By virtue of this selection the term disciple was narrowed to this group by traditional usage. During the ministry of Jesus, numerous others were designated as disciples. Those who followed Him were commonly known as "His disciples." Thus the contemporaneous description of the term has been preserved. Jesus had twelve disciples, seventy disciples, and a great multitude of disciples. There were active disciples and passive disciples, true disciples and false disciples.

Discipleship means a decision to follow Jesus Christ. It consists, in actual fact, of a determination to abandon everything so that one may follow Jesus anywhere and may accept the life and privation of a wanderer. Discipleship is not a new nomenclature; Moses had disciples (John 9:28); John had disciples (Mark 2:18); even the Pharisees had disciples (Matthew 22:16). It calls for the spirit of loving devotion and requires the giving of priority to the cause of Christ. In summary, a disciple is: (1) one who believes and trusts in Christ (2) one who learns in the school of Christ, (3) one who is committed to a sacrificial life for His sake, (Luke 14:27,33) and (4) one who acts to fulfill the climactic obligation of discipleship, namely, that of making disciples of others. (Matthew 28:19 – the imperative here is "make disciples")

New Testament discipleship was not a terminal course in teacher training. It was not a transitional stage which ended with the disciple's becoming a teacher on their own. The words of Jesus are clear: "The disciple is not above his master, nor the servant above his lord. It is enough for the disciple that he be as his master, and the servant as his lord."
"As his master" does not mean the promotion of the disciple to the rank of master, but it refers to a readiness to bear the same abuse which the teacher encountered and to ascent to as a mark of supreme distinction. (Matthew 10:24, 25)

The disciples were to have only one Master, and together all the followers of Christ were to learn from Him. This meaning of discipleship is clearly stated in the words of Jesus to some believing Jews: "If ye continue in my word, then are ye my disciples indeed." Jesus gave His Name to the disciples as their authority.

The Gospels do not teach that salvation and discipleship are two distinct things, but that they are two parts of a single experience which involves one's relationship to Jesus Christ as Savior and Lord. It is clear that Jesus taught that when one is saved he becomes a disciple (learner). The New Testament presents Jesus as both Savior and Lord and requires that He be accepted and followed.

The special relationship between Jesus and His disciples is in keeping with the special character of His teaching. The disciples must be distinguished from His followers, because disciples were a more intimate group. It is true that what He demands from disciples does not in fact differ from what He asks of everybody: to repent in the light of the coming Kingdom; to abandon everything and to follow the call; to sell all for one precious pearl. This had been the call advanced to all. The difference between the disciples and the followers can be seen in their response to the call and in the varying degrees of conviction and of loyalty.

IX. DISCIPLESHIP DEMONSTRATED

Jesus was extremely popular as long as He was healing the sick and feeding the multitudes, but when the people discovered the demands of His discipline they wanted nothing more to do with Him. It seemed that Jesus was always whittling down the multitudes that followed Him.

Those who were there for the "loaves and fishes" soon departed. The demands of discipleship were too difficult for them. One occasion, Jesus even asked the disciples who remained, "Will ye also go away?" Realizing that salvation and discipleship were bound together, they answered: "To whom shall we go? Thou hast the words of eternal life." Those who remained were willing to abide by the requirements of discipleship and could be counted on to obey the commandments of Jesus.

Discipleship means decision, but it does not mean decision to follow the crowd. Originally the term "disciple" had a much broader meaning than it has now, but it did not then include everybody who listened to Jesus teach or those who were moved enough by Him to follow along with the crowd. Discipleship is a decision to believe and to follow Jesus Christ. It means a complete decision to go all the way--commitment to complete the journey regardless of the cost.

Call to Discipleship. The call to discipleship goes forth to everyone and the response of each person is an act of obedience. Jesus is the Christ and has authority to call and to demand obedience to His Word. The seriousness of the call is demonstrated by the earliest disciples. Their encounter with Jesus was a testimony to His absolute and direct authority; Jesus called them and expected them to obey which resulted in salvation and discipleship. "Follow me simply meant that they were to forsake all and to follow in the footsteps of Jesus, not that there was glory in following but that the individual may serve as a disciple. The old things were forsaken with their relative security for that which seems to be absolute insecurity. However, complete abandonment to Christ becomes security and safety as one walks in fellowship with Jesus. An example of such commitment came from Jim Elliot's journal (1956) when five missionaries were killed by the Auca Indians in Peru. A few days before his death, Jim wrote: "He is no fool who gives up what he cannot keep to gain what he cannot lose."

Conditions of Discipleship.   Men who would follow Jesus must take certain definite steps. Discipleship is a summons for one to assume an exclusive attachment to Jesus Christ. This requires proximity and priority. The first step that follows the call, severs the individual from his previous existence and places him in a situation where faith is possible.   To take the next step, the individual must "enroll" in the school of Christ and learn to live a principled life, patterned after Christ Himself.

Jesus wanted individuals close to Him so that He could teach them by word and by deed. Only in this way would they become His disciples. There must be a strong attachment to Jesus and to His teachings. Talking intimately about the meaning and purpose of discipleship, Jesus stated that it was a matter of abiding in Him, and this abiding would be marked by receiving His word, by obeying His commands, and by loving one another. By this abiding, they would bear much fruit and would be His disciples indeed. Jesus declared that this kind of discipleship would glorify the Father in the world. (John 15:1-17)

According to the New Testament, no man can know Jesus Christ as Savior who is not willing to know Him as Lord.

Scripture is clear one must confess with the mouth the Lord Jesus and believe in the heart that God raised Christ from the dead to be saved.   What is involved in believing that God raised Jesus from the dead? He was "declared to be the Son of God with power....by the resurrection from the dead." It is simply a belief in the Sonship of Jesus Christ. The confession of Christ as Lord is involved in salvation and in discipleship. When Christ becomes Lord of one's life, He rules that life. The individual gladly bows and obeys; that is discipleship. When Jesus spoke to the multitude and placed before them the demands of discipleship, He did not hesitate to ask them to forsake all and to follow Him. He was to be their Savior and their Lord. He pointed to the cross as a mark of discipleship and as evidence of their faith.

The conditions of discipleship must never be understood as a moral code that Jesus demanded of only a few. All who would follow Christ and be His disciples must meet the same conditions.   There are no exceptions.   The conditions involved in discipleship are well illustrated in the story of the rich young ruler. The rich young man had it all: wealth, excellent character, social prominence and an earnest desire for eternal life. Yet this young man turned away from Christ deeply grieved, because he saw himself by new standards and his confidence and pride were destroyed. His past efforts to keep the law, his struggles and victories, were blotted out by a new light. They were devalued as the merest ABC of moral attainment beside the demands of Jesus to "sell all...and give...Come... follow me!" This is what all the others had to do, but it implied giving up control, total commitment, and a more intense consecration. The young man knowing fully that Jesus was the way to eternal life was unwilling to make the commitment and he went away humbled, chastened, and self-exposed.   The unwritten message is obvious... And Jesus let him go!

Cost of Discipleship. People did not follow Jesus blindly. He told them what it would cost to be His disciple. Jesus invited them to come and to take up His yoke as a mark of discipleship. Those who desired to be disciples must count the cost. It is necessary to take these steps: (1) forsake all, (2) deny self, (3) take up the cross, and (4) follow Christ. A closer look at these steps well describes a would-be disciple.

Forsake all. Jesus declared that those who would not forsake everything could not be His disciples. All conflicting loyalties must be put aside. He said exactly the same things about salvation and discipleship. The rich young man was told to "...sell all...Come...follow me." Nothing less than complete dedication was sufficient. When Jesus insisted that a man must "hate" his family, friends and possessions, He did not mean that they should despise these things. (Luke 14:26; Matthew 10:36-39). Jesus wanted his followers to have the love of a family, share the joy of friendship, and possess sufficient earthly goods to insure a happy life, but He did not want these things to stand between Him and the disciples. He demanded priority. Jesus was comparing human love to the new spiritual love the disciple would have for the heavenly Father. Compared to the human emotion and physical attachment, the spiritual love of the disciple was to be so great that all else seemed as hate. However, there are cases in which one must literally forsake all earthly attachments to assure a proper attachment to Christ, but in such cases the disciple is promised "an hundredfold" reward in this life, and in the world to come he is promised eternal life. (Matthew 19:29)

Deny Self. Denying self is accepting Jesus Christ as Lord. This is a vital part of discipleship. One must be "delivered from the body of this death." Selfish ambitions have no place in discipleship. The capital "I" in SIN is the source of most human difficulties. Many years ago S. D. Gordon aptly expressed the idea when he wrote, "In every redeemed heart there is a throne and a cross. If self is on the throne, Jesus is on the cross..." Let self be on the cross and Jesus on the throne. Self must be crucified; Christ must rule and reign.

The hymn of Frances Ridley Havergal (1874) spoke to the meaning of true discipleship:

In full and glad surrender I give myself to thee, Thine utterly and only and evermore to be.

O Son of God, who lovest me, I will be thine alone; And all I have and am, Lord, shall henceforth be thine own!

Reign over me, Lord Jesus; O make my heart thy throne: It shall be thine, dear Savior, it shall be thine alone.

O come and Reign, Lord Jesus; rule over everything! And keep me always loyal, and true to thee, my King.

Take Up the Cross. The disciple must be identified with Jesus Christ, and the cross is that identification. There is only one cross, the cross of Jesus. This is the "yoke" of which Jesus spoke, the symbol of death, and the believer must be "crucified with Christ" to become His disciple. One should not sing, "Jesus, I my cross have taken..." in reality it is "Jesus, I Thy cross have taken, all to leave and follow Thee." Taking up the cross is the disciple's way of saying "yes" to Christ and "no" to self and to the world which is the only way to be free from self. Until an individual is willing to take up the cross and to follow Jesus, he is not worthy to be a disciple.

Follow Christ. Obeying the call of Jesus means to follow Christ daily. This must be the innermost longing of the soul. Following Christ includes a desire to know Him in the Power of His resurrection and in the fellowship of His suffering. Following Christ causes the believer to be made conformable unto His death and makes one willing to take up His cross. Any who will not follow Christ and will not meet these conditions has no right to claim to be His disciple. Those who will not be a disciple have no reason to claim to be a Christian. The Christian must first be a disciple, one who follows and becomes Christ-like.

What does it mean to be a Christian? The disciples were first called Christians at Antioch. They were first of all converts and then became disciples of Christ and learners at the year long school of St. Paul and Barnabas. (Acts 11:26) Following the teachings of Christ under the tutorship of Paul and Barnabas, they became associated with the Christ-like life, and became recognized as Christians. It is tragic that many desire to be Christians but are not willing to pay the price of discipleship. These would-be disciples desire to reduce discipleship to the level of their own lives and to stipulate their own terms.

There are three such would-be disciples spoken of in Luke's Gospel (Luke 9: 57-62): The **first** would-be disciple wanted to follow Jesus without waiting to be called, and Jesus warns him that he does not understand the meaning of discipleship. The disciple is called to a life of self-sacrifice and service. Without the call of Christ, the individual would not be able to pay the price.

The **second** would-be disciple was called by Jesus to follow Him, but he wanted to bury his father first (await the death of his father). At the critical moment when Jesus calls one to follow Him nothing –not even the law itself—must act as a barrier to discipleship. The ones called must accept the absolute authority of Jesus and must follow Him without hesitation.

The **third** would-be disciple was similar to the first who offered to follow Jesus on his own initiative, but this one was bold enough to stipulate his own terms. He was not willing to give Jesus priority. He placed a barrier between Christ and himself by wanting to go first and bid farewell to his family and his friends. This was a normal thing to do, but Christ had called him and demanded first place in that life. He wanted to follow, but he felt obliged to insist on his own terms. Discipleship to him was something that he could choose for himself at his time, place, and price. This could never be Christian discipleship. These three men illustrate some of the basic problems of discipleship: hearing the call, forsaking all, denying self, counting the cost, and following Christ.

X. DISCIPLESHIP DEMANDED

The new discipline taught and lived by Jesus Christ demanded discipleship and produced two practical problems. First, one must apply the new discipline to life; second, one should find the power to accept and to put the demands into action. These are the most urgent and most practical problems. Discipleship is demanded by Jesus, and it requires a decision to follow the call.

When Christ calls one to follow Him, He expects the person to apply the new discipline personally to life. Jesus is the same and the requirements of discipleship have not changed. He still requires an exceeding righteousness. When a man is called to Discipleship, Christ Himself furnishes the strength to follow. Christ manifested amazing confidence in average men and committed into their hands the work of him Kingdom. Jesus seemed to have unwavering confidence in the people who had accepted His discipline. Jesus was certain that the growing power of His teaching on their lives and deeds would be sufficient to produce disciples of distinction for the Kingdom.

The objective of the Great Commission was the making of disciples. God, throughout history, has been in the process of teaching individuals, of making disciples, and of creating His glorious likeness within the human family. It is through these means that He is preparing them for a new world order designated as His Kingdom. One expects the followers of Christ to be busy in the world, making disciples by precept and practice.

The foundation and the function of the movement established by Jesus before His return to the Father were adequately described by the ministry of Jesus. The supreme sacrifice and the regnant resurrection of Jesus laid a deep and strong foundation for His ministry. The power of the Holy Spirit poured out at Pentecost on dedicated disciples validated His promise. The pervading presence of the Spirit brought impact and inspiration for life-style witnessing. This baffled the foes of the new discipline and finally the disciples were warned not to speak any more in the name of Jesus. This only emboldened the disciples and they continued to speak what they had seen and heard about Jesus. There was an inward fire that could not be quenched and an inner voice that could not be stilled. The message was too good to keep: salvation must be shared. The soul light of the disciples shined brightly and the name of Jesus was exalted.

Why are so many would-be disciples impotent and powerless—worshiping in churches growing numerically, but failing to grow spiritually and at times not growing at all? Why do some churches fight a losing battle? Does the Gospel have no power to transform lives and to transfer the interests of men from themselves to Jesus Christ? Is God different from what He was in the days of the Apostles? Does Jesus no longer call individuals to follow Him? Was God more concerned about the Early Church than He is about the churches today? The answer to all these questions is an emphatic "no". The church has failed to lift up Jesus as the real Savior and Lord of believers. The claims of discipleship have not been placed before the people who profess Christ. The church has secured only decisions and has stopped short of making disciples. Christian discipleship is still possible and Jesus Christ still demands it.

What is a disciple? Who should be called a Christian? A believer who learns the doctrine and discipline of Jesus and whose life is changed by Divine power can become Christ-like, but this demands discipleship. A believer who desires to live close to God and who follows Christ daily and is devoted to a life of truth and is committed to the principles of right is a disciple. When others recognize a Christ-like life-style in an individual, that person deserves to be called a Christian. The call, "Follow Me" was not made to the Twelve alone, but to each person who lives and believes on Jesus Christ. Decision is demanded; discipleship is required to become Christ-like. Each person is challenged to decide about Jesus and the discipline of His Kingdom. A choice must be made: it is discipleship or disaster. One who calls themselves a Christian without the life-style to validate their profession is an actor on a humanistic stage, a sacrilege to the church, and an open imposter and charlatan to the public.

Study and Review Questions for Section Three

1. What is discipleship:
2. How are salvation and discipleship related?
3. What does it mean to be called a Christian?
4. Why are some churches powerless and not growing?
5. What does it mean to deny self?"

DECALOGUE OF DUTY

There is no attempt in this section to present solutions to particular moral problems or to dictate in detail the behavior appropriate to every circumstance of life. Instead, this is an effort to set forth certain basic obligations that must be remembered and to which conduct must conform if one is to be considered Christ-like; thus, a Christian.

Holy Scripture does not provide a detailed list of specified rules of conduct. The Christian life is learned primarily from what other Christians live. It is taught by example, but the examples could not possibly cover every situation of life; therefore, there is an inner force in the life of a believer that becomes a guiding light toward morality and proper behavior. Ancient Scripture recorded "The spirit of man is the candle of the Lord that searches out the inward parts of his being." In the Gospels and Acts, the foundation of Christian teachings were introduced and elaborated in the Epistles. Expected conduct was exemplified in the lives of early believers. Scripture, however, gives the human family a basic formula to assure proper conduct: Jesus is to work a work in the heart and change one's nature and motivate the life force in each individual. The Holy Spirit then becomes a guide to believers enabling each one to develop a mature personality and to direct proper daily conduct.

The problems of these times must be dealt with constructively. A creative initiative must be brought to the task of Christian living based on the words and deeds of Jesus and empowered by the guiding force of the Spirit. Jesus is alive today; not only is He on the Throne in Heaven, Jesus lives in the heart of each believer who walks in truth on the straight and narrow way guided by the Spirit. These facts make Christians aware that they are not enslaved by a written code. Equally they are not left to their own devices.

Believers are living under the discipline of the New Testament and the rules of Jesus. The divine record is before the whole human race. The recorded teachings of Jesus Christ, the historical record of the Early Church, and the examples of godly individuals throughout history create the divine record for others to follow. Regardless of the examples of men and women of history, it is clear that the strongest force for right living is still the example of Jesus. Believers have the assurance of direct aid through the Spirit as they seek to understand and to apply the will of God to their affairs. Christ still leads the way. More than that, believers are given the strength to follow on the trail marked by the lives of the faithful.

Christian Obligation

The basic obligation of discipleship is that of making

Christianity visible, intelligible, and desirable. Disciples are to show that the Christian viewpoint is practical, that the Christian concept of life makes sense, and that the Christian faith is satisfying and relevant. There is no discipleship unless everything is staked on what is believed. The disciple must live the gospel that brought the good news. A theology not based on experience and testimony cannot be considered Christian.

The life of a Christian disciple should enable the world to see more clearly the working of divine grace and glory of God manifested in a transformed life. The arena of Christian service and the circumstance of each life are different, but the basic pattern of discipleship and spiritual activity is the same. Each life must manifest the work of the Master Teacher in daily deed and devotion.

Discipleship is an interpersonal relationship between God and man, and it is of value in marking this individual and the personal relationship as being valid. It should be remembered that Jesus Himself used the term and even the angel with the resurrection message said, "Go tell His disciples." The term is also used in the Book of Acts; however, the specific designation of the Twelve as His disciples later gave way to the use of the term Christian. It is noteworthy that the word disciple cannot be found in the epistles. Why was this? Was discipleship so soon to be a thing of the past? Were the disciples so Christ-like that the term Christian replaced the designation but not the discipline.

The Early Church was not far removed from the days

of Jesus and the vital facts of discipleship. The life of Paul is a good example of discipleship. The full price of discipleship was demanded even to be associated with the Christian cause in the early days of the pristine church. Most of the epistles were directed to the brethren, the saints, the believer, in their corporate capacity as churches, but discipleship is a personal matter. The writers of the epistles were concerned with the edification of the total body of believers, but this edification was to come from the personal improvement of each believer in complete devotion to Christ and the Christian way of life. This is discipleship! The first Christians had no New Testament. They worked out personal problems of faith and conduct under the inspiration of an immediate sense of discipleship to Jesus and through the guidance of the Spirit.

The Christian Ideal

The Christian ideal lies before every believer, not as a remote mountain peak, but as an ethical Everest which must be scaled by individual skill and endurance. This ideal is a narrow path on which believers may walk with Christ, guided by the Spirit, and assured of constant companionship.

The life and discipline of Jesus Christ will have constructive consequences on the behavior of believers. Jesus is the only adequate motivation to right living. Christ is the dynamic force of discipleship. Mere legalism cannot produce true disciples or Christian conduct. Jesus never intended for the Sermon on the Mount to be made into a new Pharisee-type legal system. Such legalism emphasizes the less important issues of life and ignores the weighty matters. It often bypasses such sins as pride, anger, or envy and gives the impression that the Christian life is one of staying out of trouble.

The Christian life is more than negative living; it is positive virtue flowing out of the regenerate core of the heart. Sanctification is more than mere abstinence; it is the Lordship of Christ and the rule of the Spirit. It issues forth in life, kindness, and compassion and good works humbly done. Therefore, there can be no detailed regulation of daily situations. The principle force of right must be in the heart. Mere mechanical imitation of Christ cannot produce discipleship. Christians are not sheer imitators of Christ; they are partakers of His divine nature. Believers are children of God and "joint heirs with Christ," and they participate in the work of God in the world. Peter uttered a universal prayer when he asked that "men might be partakers of the divine nature." (1 Peter 1: 4) Man has a capacity within human nature for the likeness of God. It is possible to be so united and related to Christ that His strength becomes the believer's strength for daily living.

Believers must not shrink from the Christian ideal. They must have the consecration, the dedication, and the determination to become the person they know they ought to be. If Christianity is to have meaning, it must prove itself as a force by which men can live, and in which they can find re-enforcement and support, not only in the secret chamber, but in the performance of their daily tasks in the work-a-day world.

The individual believer must realize that his responsibility is to contribute to the total Christian witness. The basic problem involved in making this contribution seems to be that of how Christians are to live and act in the various relationships of life. The believer is a new person, a citizen of a new Kingdom, but still lives in the world and must constantly associate with both the brethren of the faith and the people of the world. Earnest believers are asking disturbing questions about their responsibilities. What should the Christian's response be toward the enormous pressures and intimidations of the world?

The principles of discipleship must be applied by the individual to daily life situations. This is often a difficult task, because it speaks of duty, a word which has some objections. In popular usage the word "duty" carries the thought of strain or constrain; however, Christian duty should be a delight. Doing one's duty should be regarded as a privilege rather that a burden. Love of the right and of the good can transform the whole idea of moral obligation, making duty a delight. Those who perform duties with sincerity and willingness transform their obligations into victories and afterwards feel the "answer of a good conscience toward both God and man."

It is true that man's destiny lies beyond this life and that this world of probation is to prepare man for the hereafter. Yet Christianity is intensively practical, touching the daily life of Man at every point. The first part of this book was concerned primarily with Man's chief responsibility— fellowship with God. Attempts were made to answer these questions: how can the broken relationship between

God and Man be restored? How can reconciliation be effected, and on what basis can Man be acceptable in the sight of God? Finding a way to God and living in constant communion with Jesus Christ has been the basic objective to this point, even though certain aspects of the Christian's relationship with others were discussed. Now the concern is with the believer's daily life as a result of this fellowship with Jesus Christ. What influence does it have on the daily affairs of believers?

Consider the ten basic obligations of Man (mankind, humankind): duty to God, to self, to family, to church, to brethren, to neighbor, to enemy, to sinner, to state, and to the world.

XI. DUTY TO GOD

The whole duty of a person is summarized in one's duty to God. All obligations are duties to God. One's duties to himself and to his fellow humans blend and overlap and are a part of his obligation to God. The essence of a person's spiritual obligation is summed up in Ecclesiastes: (1) "Fear God, and (2) keep His commandments." (Ecclesiastes 12:13) The "fear of God" is the definition of true religion in the Old Testament and means a reverence and trust in God combined with a hatred of all that is evil. Fear is the beginning of wisdom, the secret of uprightness, and the distinguishing factor of the people who give God pleasure. (Psalm 111:10; Proverbs 8:13; Psalm 147:11). The fear of God causes one to keep God's commandments. The Prophet Micah gave these words on the subject of religious responsibility: "He has shewed thee, O man, what is good;

and what doth the Lord require of thee but to do justly, and to love mercy, and to walk humbly with thy God?" (Micah 6:8)

The primary duty of Mankind is to love God. They must (1) recognize God as the Eternal Father, (2) obey and serve God, and (3) worship and trust God. The commandment of primary obligation is in both the Old and New Testaments. (Deuteronomy 6:5; Matthew 22:37, 38) The first commandment is to "love the Lord thy God..." This principle of primary obligation is taught by Jesus and the Apostle Paul. (Matthew 6:33; 1 Corinthians 10:31)

Recognize God

The Scripture presupposes God's eternal existence and, therefore, makes no effort to validate its truth. However, there is ample evidence to convince the inquiring mind that there is an eternal Deity. Being convinced of God's existence is an act of faith; once one musters this faith it logically follows that an individual must recognize God in the affairs of life.

Man's recognition of God, the Eternal Father, can be illustrated by the father-son relationship. No man could live in his father's house and not recognize the paternal interests and care. A worthy son would not eat at his father's table, share his bounty, and then ignore the father day after day by never speaking, not showing any sign of appreciation or affection to him. When the father is recognized for his paternal care, he will be honored and revered by the faithful son. There will be love, gratitude, and devotion to motivate the son's affection toward the father. These facts can easily be applied to a person's relationship with God, the Heavenly Father.

When an individual recognizes God as the Heavenly Father, reverence, respect, and repentance are logical consequences. Confronted by the power and holiness of God, one is "naked" and aware of a sinful nature. This awareness of sin brings about godly sorrow and a humble request for God's intervention into one's affairs. This divine intervention comes by faith and brings about salvation. And with salvation comes an anticipation of eternal fellowship with God.

Obey and Serve God

Aware of the knowledge of sins forgiven, Man must actively seek the will of God, and once they know this will, joyously do it. God reveals His will to obedient hearts. As the believer walks the way of obedience, he discovers that doing the will of God is best for all concerned. When a man obeys God, he commits himself to do God's will. This conception of obedience means that the divine will becomes an active, dynamic force in one's life. It is clear that obedience implies service to God.

The power to discharge the obligations of life and to do spiritual service does not lie within the individual. No amount of education, training, or experience can adequately suffice to enable Man to give God that which is the divine requirement. These things will most assuredly help, but they are not sufficient within themselves. There is no spiritual power in the flesh. The secret of spiritual service is in the willingness of one to obey God. A person can live a righteous life and discharge moral duties when they live a life of obedience to the will of God.

Man can do nothing to put himself in right relationship with God. Rather, the grace of God must be the starting point. Life must be lived from God outward. There must be earnestness toward God that seeks guidance and assistance. When these are present in the heart of Man, the duties to God are no more a terrifying demand. They become the rule of life which the believer embraces with devotion and delight.

Worship and Trust God

Obeying and serving God naturally leads one to the worship of God. Worship has to do with the worth of God in one's life. Believers must see this worth in every area of life and honor God and pursue the divine will and purpose. Walking sincerely before God in an attitude of worship is essential to doing God's will and enjoying spiritual health. God is adored and exalted by a consistent life of devotion, pure thoughts and prayer, systematic Bible study, sincere meditation, service, public worship, and serious daily living.

Worship involves responding to the worth of God and trusting God. The disciples of Jesus were taught to pray: "Thy will be done." (Matthew 6:10) Trusting God is inherently beautiful and something seems basically wrong about a person refusing to trust God. One who worships the eternal God shall be able to defend the faith with confidence, bear the chastisements of God without murmuring, and rejoice in the hope of eternal fellowship with God.

XII. DUTY TO SELF

The fact that self is placed second in treatment is deliberate. Duty to God involves obligations to self and to others, but one cannot fulfill this spiritual obligation to others until he has first established a proper relationship with the eternal God. The basic obligation is to give himself to God and to be concerned about his own spiritual welfare. Some would prefer the order of God, others, and self; some use the acrostic J-O-Y meaning Jesus first, others second and you last. This is bad logic.

Experiencing Christ is a selfish experience. One must see personal worth and value and that the individual is worth saving before one will bring themselves to repentance that brings salvation. In fact, although the Spirit draws individuals to God, the person must, in reality, bring himself to God and ask for redemption. Then, with this connection firmly established, he will be adequately prepared to take care of the spiritual needs of his family and friends. This admonition is definite: "Take heed unto thyself." (2 Timothy 4:16; 1 Corinthians 11:28; 2 Corinthians 13:5)

Self-Respect
The fact that Humans are the foremost of God's creation implies that God put the divine impress upon each individual so that each person has intrinsic worth. Each person must see their own worth. The dignity of humans is expressed in their divine origin, their upright position, their graceful form and movement, and in the fact that they can possess inner character that guides their life. The body of a human houses a spiritual being that is eternal. This soul

is worth more than the world. This fact should give each person a certain degree of self-respect and cause them to regard themselves as an individual who is capable of accomplishment under God's direction.

Self-Development

The capacity and capabilities given to Mankind by God requires them to develop and to improve. There are four basic areas of self-development: mental, physical, spiritual, and social. The knowledge that Jesus had this same fourfold development should be sufficient impetus for the believer's self-improvement. (Luke 2:52)

Mental. The Christian is encouraged to develop mental powers. The capacity for learning is a gift from God and should be used for God's glory. Consecrated brain power can mean the difference between success and failure in this enlightened age. Scripture warns that Man will learn, but never come to the full knowledge of the truth. It is evident, that one should carefully choose the facts to be learned. The believer is obligated to develop mentally to the best advantage of God's cause in the world. (2 Timothy 2:15; 1 Timothy 4:13) The development should come in at least these areas:

(a) Basic knowledge
(b) Understanding
(c) Memory and Reflection
(d) Power of the will

Physical. Living in the body that God has given, one becomes conscious of the world of creation. Humans have the capacity to learn to control and to regulate the body in which they live. It should be pointed out that no natural passion or appetite is wrong of its own nature. They are given for a good and useful purpose in the life of Mankind. However, the perversion and abuse of any physical appetite is grossly sinful and injurious to both physical and spiritual health and therefore, unnatural usage of any of these desires must be condemned. Nature seems to place a stamp of approval on the moderate and orderly use of natural forces. Man is told to"glorify God in his body," because it is God's. (1 Corinthians 6: 19, 20)

The physical house of humans is a marvelous mechanism of divine origin, made for a wise and noble purpose—to glorify God the Creator. The human body is superior to all other organisms of the earth and should have respect and dignity. The Christian understanding is that the body is to be the temple of the Spirit. The body of itself is not evil and must not be viewed as the seat of defilement. Sin is the source of evil in the universe and the body is evil only when it is an instrument of sin. The Christian, however, believes that the blood of Jesus can redeem one from the curse of sin and make the "vilest sinner clean."

A person has an obligation to preserve physical health. Anointed physical health can become spiritual energy and Man-power consecrated and harnessed by God becomes the force that moves the world toward God. Here are four ways to preserve physical health:

(a) Cleanliness of body and mind.
(b) Proper food and drink.

(c) Adequate physical exercise including work and play.

(d) Proper rest and relaxation.

Spiritual. The believer is required to learn of Jesus and to grow in grace and knowledge. The physical, mental, and social areas of self-development relate directly to the spiritual. It is evident that a stronger body, a better developed mental capacity, and harmonious social relations can contribute to the well-being of the spiritual man. It is also true that a properly developed spiritual life will affect the individual's health, mental attitude, and social life.

Social. Humans are by nature social creatures and are obligated to develop this part of life. An effort must be made to live in harmony with all people. The social side of Man's development may seem contrary to the spiritual life. This is not necessarily true. It depends on which is developed first. Provided the example of Jesus is followed— mental, physical, spiritual and then social development— the social area can be an asset to the Christian life. To care adequately for the social needs, the individual must first have a proper development of the mind, body, and the spiritual life.

The spiritual life will produce harmonious social relations. Jesus was the friend of sinners, but this friendship had a spiritual motivation. (More on the subject of Man's relationship with others can be found in Section Two, VII. DIALOGUE—MAN WITH MAN page 34)

Balance and Self-Development

There must be a balance among these areas of self-development: (1) In the physical there must be a balance between work and rest; neither must suffer at the expense of the other. (2) The mental development should have a balance between study, or gathering information, and the use of these facts in answering questions or solving problems that relate to life and service. (3) In the realm of the spiritual, there ought to be a balance between profession and practice. The spiritual development should be such as would bring about balance between such contrasting elements as firmness and kindness, faith and works, worship and service, hearing and doing. The spiritual must first be motivated by New Testament principles and Christian consideration of self and others from which the practical and proper action will issue spontaneously. (4) In the area of social development, the balance must be between perfecting one's personality and the cultivation of friendship with others. This self-development and social improvement must then be used to the spiritual advantage of all concerned.

Self-Preservation

There is a physical and a spiritual law of self-preservation. This is a law that preserves oneself from destruction, injury, and loss. In the physical realm this law seems to be an instinct or a natural law common to all human beings, but in the spiritual an awareness of this law must be developed. Humankind has the basic capacity for a spiritual law of self-preservation, but for it to be useful to one's spiritual life it must be diligently cultivated with a proper spiritual understanding of self and the spiritual nature.

The spiritual law is developed from the basic obligation of priority that the Christian must give to the Kingdom. It produces a desire to protect one's spiritual nature from injury, loss or ultimate destruction by the forces of evil in the world. This spiritual law, once it is cultivated in the heart, will cause a person to set aside anything that disrupts communion with God or weakens the appetite for the Word of God, or dilutes the desire for spiritual worship, or dulls the concern for the welfare of self or others.

An individual must remember to take heed to oneself first. One has an obligation to a personal spiritual life. Salvation and discipleship are personal matters between mankind and God, and nothing should be allowed to interfere with the personal relationship with God.

XIII. DUTY TO FAMILY

The family is a divine institution, but it is not exclusively a Christian one. The family unit can be found in all cultures, but the Christian experience and the Christian way of life have made the family a Christian institution.

Marriage and Church and State
Normally, in the Christian sector of society, marriage is a holy institution resting on divine ordinance and will. (Genesis 1:27, 28; 2:18) The Christian concept of marriage is a strict monogamy partnership based on the existence of genuine personal love and a mutual desire to live together permanently in the enjoyment of a loving relationship. The divine ideal is one man and one woman for life, yet about fifty percent of all marriages fail and many others are in a state of malfunction.

Marriage is considered an honorable safeguard against immorality, a proper means of propagating the race, and a wholesome environment in which to care for the next generation. Marriage is sanctioned by the State and blessed by the Church, but that alone does not make it a Christian venture. The permanence of Christian marriage between two people is based on a moral purpose and never on physical attraction. (Matthew 19:3-6) Marriage is a venture into a new kind of life and a new arrangement of priorities. There are risks and inevitable disillusionment unless both parties work at the relationship. However, when two people agree in love to live for Christ and each other, they can receive strength to solve the daily problems.

The church is a powerful re-enforcement to the true meaning of marriage; however, even love needs training and discipline to be wisely expressed. (Titus 2:4-8) For this reason, the wedding vows are repeated in the church before a minister with the understanding that this validation is part of the joint commitment to a relationship. A Christian marriage takes for granted that both the husband and the wife will actively participate in the spiritual life of the church and consequently keep God in the marriage picture. It is common sense to understand that marriage should be between persons of similar religious convictions (2 Corinthians 6:14). One should remember that marriage is also a civil contract between two parties and that a contract may be broken by either party. Failure on the part of either of the contracting parties to live up to this expectation will have grave consequences. "Can two walk together, except they be agreed?"

Christian Home: Marriage between believers is expected to establish a Christian home into which children will be born, loved, and brought up in the fear and the admonition of the Lord. The New Testament presents the ideal Christian home and implies that the whole of human relationships are to be influenced by following Jesus Christ.

Christ Claims Authority: Jesus claims absolute supremacy over all of life. He must have authority in the home. The initial requirements of discipleship cannot be abandoned. Jesus must motivate the family life and the agenda of each member. The obligation of believers to any person is limited or enforced by the supreme obligation to Jesus Christ. This obligation is greater than that of wife to husband, child to parent, or servant to master. All harmonious relationships in these areas are approved by Jesus, but He claims first place in the heart of each family member. Nothing must come between Jesus and those who follow Him. Contrary to the thinking of some persons, there can be no two people closer in human love that those who have both given themselves completely to Christ. This is the secret of supreme happiness in the home of a Christian.

Christian Attitude: The Christian experience creates an attitude toward others and governs the relationship of each member of the family to the other members. Once the self has been committed to God it can never be pre-eminent again. God is first and having placed His love within the believer, there will be a Christian attitude toward others. Remember, an attitude is a predisposition to act. When each member of the family recognizes Jesus Christ as the Supreme Being, they will find their relationship toward each other ennobled and purified as they enjoy the multiplied blessings of a Christian home.

A most glorious picture of the Christian home is presented in the writings of the Apostle Paul, a man who for the cause of Christ gave up the joys of such a life. However, it is evident that Paul understood the simplicity and the beauty of the Christian home. He was primarily concerned with the Christian life in the family institution, and he pictured this ideal.

Christian Family Relationships
A general introduction to the subject of family relationship is given in these words of Paul: "And whatsoever ye do in word or deed, do all in the name of the Lord Jesus, giving thanks to God and the Father by him." (Colossians 3:17)   Paul believed that to relate oneself to another in the name of Jesus meant to do so "in His power" or "as belonging to Him." Even simple family relationships are to be determined on the basis of the believer's belonging to Christ

A table of duties for the members of the family appear in Paul's writings. (Colossians 3:18-4:1; Ephesians 5:21-6:9) He placed emphasis on order, obedience, subordination, and respect for authority. Paul's comments on the family relationship seem to be an elaboration on the fact that the Christian life is lived in the midst of the common duties of life.

Husband and Wife: The relationship between husband and wife is a figure of the relationship between Christ and the church. The ideal of true love is expressed in Ephesians: "Husbands, love your wives, even as Christ also loved the church..." The order of things by virtue of creation would suggest that the wife was to be subject to her husband. This does not mean being in bondage. Paul is careful to make certain that the subjection of wife to husband is regulated by the Christian formula: "in the Lord". When the husband loves with the love of Christ, the wife's love is realized and finds its highest manifestation in submission. This is not a negative word; it simply means to line up under different authority. Prior to marriage the wife was lined up under the authority of her father; therefore, with the marriage vow, she was to line up under a different arrangement as it related to her husband.

Problems in married life are to be settled by the force of the partner's personal Christian faith. The husband-wife relationship is to be maintained until the death of one of the partners, except in extreme circumstances. In marriages consummated before conversion, the believer is to make fervent effort to convert the other partner to the faith and thus establish a Christian home. "Dwell... giving honor...as being heirs together of the grace of life; that your prayers be not hindered." (1 Peter 3:7)

Paul presented the ideal, but discipleship is often maintained in different and difficult circumstances. At times there is only one who serves Christ and the ideal home situation is marred by this division. The position of the disciple in such a case is indeed difficult, but the grace of God is sufficient. (See the Triangle Relationship Figure on page 37.)

Responsibility of Parents: There must be a joint

assumption of certain responsibilities in marriage. The husband and wife, as parents, have responsibilities to each other and to their children. The paternal responsibility is clearly stated in Paul's word: "And, ye fathers provoke not your children to wrath: but bring them up in the nurture and admonition of the Lord." Children are to be tenderly trained and disciplined in a manner so as not to gender resentment to the parents' authority. "Train up a child," best expresses the individual responsibility of the parent to each child.

The religious responsibility of parents includes: family devotions and prayer, regular public worship, and consistent Christian living. The whole family ought to attend the church services together and readily discuss the spiritual truth learned and the blessings experienced. The abandonment of these age-old customs is a tragic reality in many modern homes and the results can only be determined by time and eternity.

The home of the Christian should be conducive to spiritual progress. Scripture is explicit that the home is the practical center for the teaching of spiritual matters. The home has first and foremost influence in the life and development of the child. It is there that the child is best understood and most loved. The Christian home gives opportunity for worship, education, discipline, moral example and leadership. Life's basic concepts are determined in the home by clear moral and ethical teaching, the example of godly parents, and the loving atmosphere of family fellowship.

The church was established to aid the home in its high

function.   Here the family worships together and is ministered to from the Word of God. The home is no longer the center of family activity. A child is born in a hospital, fed out of a bottle, raised in a nursery, clothed by a factory, schooled by the public, entertained by the crowd, and often neglected by the parents to pursue their own selfish agenda. The home should be a sacred place, but little provision is made for the spiritual well-being of the modern family. The busy world leaves little time for parents to prepare themselves or their families to face life's problems. Instead the "entertainment age" has taken over. The family is pulled toward an artificial happiness rather than the deep contentment that spiritual maturity can produce. For example:

A recent ad in a family magazine went something like this: Take family night to a whole new level. Your family can earn a PhD in fun. Grab the kids, invite over the neighbors and turn your living room into a campus of higher hilarity. School each other in the art of thinking quick with a multitude of micro-challenges that flex your mental muscles and your funny bone. It's Family Fun 101 and it's on your TV.

Although it is important for the family to have fun together in a variety of ways, it is vital for parents to realize that "happiness" is not always possible.   There are responsibilities to consider.

The church must assume an active role in the preparation of the family for life and death. The church should guide the parents through the educational program and regular worship services. The family and the home ought to be a vital part of the total ministry of the church.

Child and Parent: This is a tender and intimate relationship and is a God-created connection that is so grand and glorious until it is usually not properly appreciated until it has passed. The beauty of a tender child influenced by a godly parent is portrayed throughout the Bible. Jesus was displeased with anyone who refused to take time to help children enter the Kingdom. He declared that children belonged in His Kingdom. (Luke 18:15-17)

The child is to learn obedience to parents as preparation for obeying the divine will in later life. Any child who does not learn to respect parental authority will not likely respect any kind of authority, civil or divine.

Family, Community, and Church

God ordered and God ordained three basic institutions: family, community, and church. The State is a part of the community authority and is not an entity in the original construct of mankind. The State is Man-made, developed out of the community authority as are other aspects of society: business, government, education, etc. The basic institutions shown in Figure 4 all relate directly to the individual. God is concerned about the individual while mankind seems more concerned about the group. In a collective sense, these institutions were designed to produce, protect and preserve the individual. When the social structures fail to demonstrate basic concern for the individual, the purpose of God is thwarted.

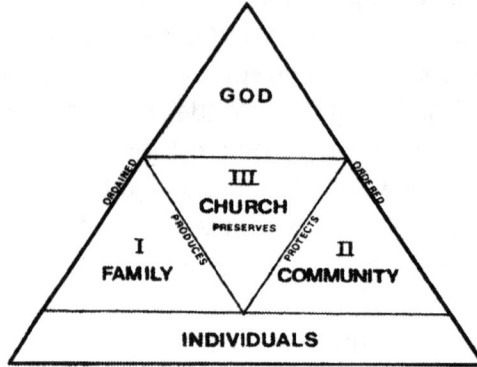

Figure 4 – Basic Institutions are related to the Individual. A Higher Power reaches the individual in the context of these institutions. All institutions must work within these boundaries to be effective.

Basic Understanding of Institutions

Understanding how human beings function in families, groups, and organizations is a precondition to creating an atmosphere conducive to learning and spiritual development. A foundational philosophy of life begins with three basic institutions. These institutions were ordained and ordered by Divine Providence. They are the **established family, constituted community authority,** and the **organized church.** Leadership must clearly comprehend that the primary concern of Divinity was individual welfare. When concern for individual rights and justice is placed on the back burner in order to increase bottom line profits, evil is apparent in the process. In a Christian environment, an individual can never become just a number to be discarded or dealt with arbitrarily. Of course, there are times when behavior violates accepted culture and eliminates an individual from productive development. In such case, the parents and teachers must function for the good of the whole.

Institutions and Individuals

Each institution was initiated for the good of the individual. These three fundamental institutions are interrelated and cannot survive alone. God ordered and ordained that individuals should be **produced** within an established family, **protected** in a constituted community, and **preserved** in the context of both family, constituted community, and in an organized church.

The family produces individuals within the framework of Divine order and the established laws of society. When individuals are born without the care and nurture of a loving two-parent family, many problems are inflicted on the community as a whole. Some of these difficulties become evident in the life of organizations and institutions.

The family is the first and most basic of the institutions and it molds the lives of children before school, church, and state exert extensive influence on them. For this reason, it is most important. The family is of paramount importance in the life of each individual. No Christian service that is contradicted by the life in the family is of value. Modern society often neglects the family in favor of multiplied engagements. This seems to be the spirit of the times.

Constituted community authority protects individuals. In this effort, the community even protects the guilty from the wrath of individuals. Yet, the community is structured to punish individuals who violate the conventional wisdom of community authority. Organizational life must consider both the protection of the individual and the separation of those individuals who would harm the community.

God ordained and ordered the **organized church to preserve individuals** within the context of the family and the community. It is within the family that the church receives members and the community provides opportunity for service and outreach. The individual members of the church have a role in both functions. Parents are to dwell together in harmony so their prayers will not be hindered. Partners in marriage are obligated to separate each other from participation in the evils of the community lest their children become defiled. Yet, each individual is responsible to God, the church, the community, and the family to conduct their life in keeping with stated moral and ethical standards. When these standards are broken everyone suffers including all the basic institutions: family, community, and the church.

XIV. DUTY TO THE CHURCH

The life of Jesus is the force of the Christian faith. Jesus had an eternal effect on the lives and deeds of people. They forsook all, denied themselves, took up the cross, and followed Jesus to their death. Not only what Jesus began to do and to teach in the Gospels changed lives, but what Jesus continued to do and to teach through the "Church" (a fellowship of all who found union with God and who would bring the reality of Jesus Christ into all their living). Consecrated, Spirit-filled lives of the Early Church transformed individuals into Christian disciples.

Everything dear to the heart of Jesus is tied up in the Church and its work in the world. The New Testament knew nothing of "free lance" Christianity. The believers were united for personal edification and Christian witness. A holy love bound them together as a resolute band of believers determined to change the world for good.

The Church ministered to various needs of the individual for personal edification, and each believer contributed to the effectiveness of the total Christian witness. Exerting Christian influence was the result of a united effort of all believers to live for Christ in the world. To accomplish this influence, each believer had to maintain a personal relationship with Christ as a present experience.

The purpose of the church is to maintain Christian ideals, to edify believers, to reach the lost, and to be a moral influence in the world. The church is weak today, despite numerical strength, because members often expect the corporate image to be a sufficient influence on society. The organized church cannot do the task that has been assigned to individual believers. Practical thinking is personal. The church is only the aggregate of all its members and cannot be better than the spiritual experience of those who compose it.

Nothing effectively can be done as long as the church is thought of as a whole. It is a fallacy of division to reason that what is true of the whole is true of the part. The churches, with all their purity and power, can never by published standards alone, influence the world. The faith and the standards of the "Church" must be exemplified in the lives of individual members. Discipleship is an individual matter just as salvation is a personal experience. Christ is the Builder of the Church, and while it is true that the organized church contributes to the Christian life of individuals, the world is influenced by the personal experience and testimony of believers. The individual believer is a vital part of the church, but the witness of the "Church" is determined by how the individual members conduct themselves in their affairs with others.

Church Membership

The Christian must seek to understand the ministry of the organized church, its place and purpose in each member's life, and to attach himself to it with intelligence and loyalty as an earnest member. The duty of the Christian to belong to a congregation is involved in personal duty to: Christ, oneself, fellow Christians, and the world. Membership in a congregation enlightens the believer to the Christian obligations and provides strength to fulfill this duty.

The believer must not only be attached to Christ, there must also be a union with other believers. The abiding influence of the church is essential to maintain the proper relationship with God. Scripture clearly teaches that the Christian experience is strengthened by believer fellowship and weakened by the lack of it. An alliance with other believers in the worship and work of the church assures continued fellowship with Christ.

Church membership is limited to those who meet certain requirements set forth in Scripture. Anyone who does not meet the qualifications of personal salvation and a willingness to walk in the light of the Scripture cannot become a member of the True Church. Membership, however, is a logical step for the converted person. Love and devotion to Jesus Christ will naturally cause one to associate with others who share the same attachment. The Church is that divine institution that Jesus loved and sacrificed Himself to establish. It has a holy mission and a sacred message. It is natural for the followers of Christ to love and desire its fellowship.

There is little security for the believer outside the protection and influence of Christian fellowship. God's plan did not leave the convert to face the "wiles of the devil" alone. The church was established to provide a place of divine refuge and is the believer's God-given sanctuary. Membership in this blessed institution is important. Through the Word of God and constant Christian companionship, the believer gains strength and courage to meet life's most trying times. Every convert to the Christian faith belongs within this great company of believers. The spiritual life is impaired when fellowship is lacking. Personal Christian experience could not long exist in these last days without participation in this vital part of God's plan.

Consistent Worship

Being a member of the church involves attendance at worship services and full participation in the life of the congregation with thankfulness and persistence. Membership responsibilities include: being faithful to God, living a clean moral life, remaining loyal and steadfast in faith, doing Christian service, assembling together and encouraging one another. (Colossians 3:15, 16) Participation in spiritual activity should bring the member into the presence of God.

In Creation, God gave man a mind with which to think, a heart with which to love, a will with which to choose, and a soul which would be desirous of worship and fellowship. Of all God's creation, man alone possesses the capacity and desire to worship God. Worship is that necessary nourishment and pleasure the spiritual man needs to grow in grace. In fact, worship is acknowledging the worth-ship of God and the value of the God-Man relationship.

People can worship God anywhere at anytime, but generally they worship best in groups. Group activity becomes less satisfying as the group becomes larger. This should be a warning to the super-church. To survive, large congregations must have many small groups active in the life of the church: strong family emphasis, effective classes, prayer groups, study groups, youth groups, fellowship groups, and other such groups and activities as needed in the community.

Individuals who fail to participate in public worship usually will not have the desire or the strength to maintain family devotions or personal meditation and prayer in the home. The believer has an obligation to God, oneself, the family, and the church to be consistent in public worship. Active participation in the life of the church is necessary to keep membership meaningful. Without regular attendance interest will decline and the Christian unity of the believer with others will deteriorate. When the frequency of attendance and participation decreases, a decrease in the strength of the fellowship will follow. As a result, members seem to become "neutral" in their feelings toward one another. Even when the Early Church was meeting almost daily, the writer of Hebrews warned against "forsaking the assembling of ourselves together." An additional injunction followed; "And so much the more as ye see the day approaching." Gathering together with other believers will keep the worship of God and the vital fellowship of the church alive.

Worship must be the motivating force of church attendance. A Christian test of worship causes the believer to ask: "Does my church attendance make me more Christ-like in attitude and behavior?" Church attendance or merely being a spectator at a worship service is not enough. Church attendance must be used for the true worship of God and should never become a substitute for personal worship. Participating ought to re-enforce the believer 's Christian behavior. This is suggested when Jesus spoke of a man who brought his gift to the altar and remembered that he and his brother were in disagreement. Jesus declared that this worshiper must first be reconciled to his fellow man and then his worship would have meaning, and God would receive his gift at the altar. (Matthew 5:23, 24)

Cheerful Support

God has ordained that the church should be supported and sustained by the moral and material interests of its membership. God's principle of personal, regular, free-will, cheerful giving is clearly set forth in Scripture. Christian giving is not a matter of law, but rather of grace. The illustration of liberality is the sacrificial offering of a widow who gave her living while the rich gave tokens from their wealth. Once the believer catches the spirit of

Christian stewardship, the greatest joy is participating in the privilege of giving. A motivation is the spirit of Christ who gave His all.

Returning one-tenth to God's work was emphasized in the Old Testament. However, the law of the tithe has not been abolished or repealed and still carries with it an abundant blessing. Tithing has been accepted in the New Testament as a lesson learned by example. This rule of returning one-tenth has stood the test of time and experience. The Jews were blessed by the practice of tithing, and the principle of giving has become the basis of the Christian's material obligation to the ministry of the church.

Consider a brief history of the tithe: Abraham commenced it (Genesis 14:18-20); Jacob continued it (Genesis 28:20-22); Moses confirmed it (Leviticus 27:30-34); Malachi commanded it (Malachi 3:10); Jesus commended it (Luke 11:42); many faithful believers still practice it. An effective statement concerning tithing and giving was made by W. L. Prichard to the student body at Mercer University:

Give the first-tenth to the Lord. Use the next eight-tenths for the obligations of life. Save the last-tenth and you will always have something for love offerings. Whoever follows this formula will have the high satisfaction of the respect of God and man.

When a Christian gives to support the ministry of the church, it should be given in the right spirit. It should be a privilege to give to the Christian cause. All gifts should come from a heart of love. The story of the poor widow and her two mites tells of this full measure of devotion. She gave her all into the treasure of the lord. The gift was measured by what the widow had left and therefore the gift was considered greater than the gifts of the rich men whose purses remained full.

A gift is measured in terms of the giver. It is not the size of the gift but the spirit of the giver that counts with God. A gift is measured by what it costs the giver – by what the giver has left. The sacrifice to the individual is the determining factor. Giving has been defined as "the unselfish outpouring of yourself in substance." It is the willing gift of one's possessions, with no return expected, that determines the measure of a gift and the reward to the giver.

A record of true love gifts to the work of the church is found in the Apostle Paul's counsel to the Corinthians to abound in the grace of liberality. Their example was the poor Macedonians who first gave themselves to God and then out of their deep poverty gave liberally to the work of the ministry. The church would not want for support if all members followed Paul's advice: "Upon the first day of the week let everyone of you lay by him in store, as God hath prospered him." The Christian is obligated to regularly support the ministry of the church in proportion to personal prosperity.

Consider the Scriptural method of giving: without show (Matthew 6:3); regularly in proportion (1 Corinthians 16:2); liberally and cheerfully (2 Corinthians 9:7); and sacrificially (2 Samuel 24:24). The true spirit of worship creates in one a desire to give of self and of resources to God in consecrated service. Participation increases one's inspiration for any effort. Those who know the most about God's work and participate fully in the activity of the church are the recipients of greater blessings and happiness.

Christian Living

The primary obligation of the believer to the church is to live a Christian life and uphold the New Testament standard of Christianity. The Christian must take care to correlate worship of God with the circumstances of everyday life. A re-enforcement for Christian living must come from worship, and Christian living should strengthen the desire for worship. If Christians are called to a life of holiness, it is because Jesus has made it possible. Those who dare to believe can experience in their heart and demonstrate to others the reality of Christian living.

The consecrated Christian life is characterized by self-denial and complete devotion to the cause of Christ. Jesus demanded discipleship and the church has the right to expect the believer to follow Christ daily. The Christian demonstrates discipleship through loyalty to the church. Believers must stand against wrong and stand for the right and live positively seeking to promote the principles of the New Testament through daily living.

The Christian is obligated to "walk worthy of God." When the Word of God is preached, the believer must receive and obey the Word. Notice these words of Paul:

That ye would walk worthy of God, who hath called you unto his Kingdom and glory. For this cause also thank we God without ceasing, because, when ye received the word of God which ye heard of us, ye received it not as the word of men, but as it is in truth, the word of God, which effectually worketh also in you that believe. (1 Thessalonians 2:12, 13).

When the believer worships God, He speaks directly in many ways. The Christian must lay aside all preconceived notions and let the Word effectively work in the heart. When the Word does an effective work in the heart, the believer will go forth living the Word by life and lip. Believing is to help being. Doctrine is to make discipleship. Creed is to fashion character. Christian convictions constitute a call to be a true witness of the truth in life.

Christian Service

The church cannot fulfill its God-given task without believers whose lives have been changed and consecrated to Christian service. The church needs individuals who will outlive, out suffer, and outwork the world and who will be a "burning and a shining light" for the Christian cause. The church should have unquestioned priority in the life of the Christian. Social and community activities, worthy as they may be, must take their chance with the remaining time.

Christian discipleship demands service. The believer must joyously search for God's will in a program of outgoing love and service. Believers should be busy in the service of the Lord. To live close to God, the believer must follow Christ in humble ways of service and stand in the presence of God, ready and willing o be sent to do God's work regardless of the circumstances. Individuals have different abilities, but each believer must employ God-given talents for the best interest of the Christian cause. Believes must work on joint projects in a united effort to advance the church and its ministry. Every area of a person's life should be viewed as a prospective place for Christian service.

Christian service will cause the believer to participate in wholesome community activities, but this participation is always in the capacity as a Christian. The believer is a representative of the church and should endeavor to make the church so evidently a place of love and service that it would be gratefully welcomed in the life of the community. The dedicated Christian should pray for the opportunity and for the courage to positively influence for Christ every segment of community life.

XV. DUTY TO THE BROTHERHOOD

A neglected aspect of the Christian's responsibility is the neglect of a duty to those believers within the Christian fellowship--the brotherhood, whether man or woman. The whole body of believers, who profess the same faith and share fellowship within the church, have obligations to one another. To belong to the church is not only to be a part of the brotherhood, but to belong is to share in the total Christian obligation. The Apostle Peter declared: "Honor all men. Love the brotherhood. Fear God. Honor the king."(1 Peter 2:17)

The best definition of a true church is "a fellowship." The Early Church influenced the known world, not only by its fresh teachings, but with its strange and unusual fellowship. An amazed and startled world could not comprehend the Christian's love for one another. Membership carried as its essence a sense of belonging one to another and involved a sense of sharing. The believers were characterized by "gladness and singleness of heart."

Believers today must have that kind of fellowship, that sense of belonging, of loving, of sharing. Fellowship, in the New Testament meaning, is an important part of the Church's existence. However, "fellowship" does not seem to be an adequate translation of the Greek, *koinonia,* used to describe the togetherness of believers. The term means a close spiritual relationship between the believer and God, but is widened to describe the spiritual uniting one with the other and indicates the common life of the community of believers. There is an evident meaning of mutual interdependence and responsibility among the believer. *Koinonia* in its fullest meaning is a comprehensive description of the unique life of the brotherhood and is fundamentally concerned with participation in things in which others also participate.

Christians must show themselves before the world as true brethren. Believers are called to fellowship and to spiritual unity. Christian fellowship should produce a heart throb, a concern, a vital interest, and a sincere helpfulness among the brotherhood. All the duties of the believer to the church are also obligations to fellow Christians. The believer's primary duty to the brotherhood is that of living an exemplary life of love and of service.

A Life of Love

A soul-shaking personal experience brings believers into one body: "So we, being many are one body in Christ and everyone members of another." (Romans 12:5; 1 John 4:7-21) Each member of the body has its function, and each function is necessary for the harmonious development of the whole. This is true of the relationship between the believer and the brotherhood. It speaks of individual obligation to the whole body of believers. The believer is obligated to live a life of love.

Jesus commanded: "That ye love one another, as I have loved you. " He also stated that His disciples would be known because they "have love one to another." Paul prayed for the Thessalonian believers "To increase and abound in love one toward another, and toward all men." Paul declared that this love would establish their hearts in holiness before God. (John 13:34, 35; 1 Thessalonians 3:12)

Inner Character of the Life

The best way to analyze the nature of brotherly love is to observe it in action. There are certain characteristics that should be expressed in a life of love toward the brotherhood. The believer's action toward the brethren should express the nature of the spiritual life.

Sincerity. The Christian must live a blameless life of holiness. There should always be transparent honesty in all relations. No pretense or imitation should be exhibited. The spiritual life among the brethren must come from within with the external actions being the manifestation of this inner life. Sincerity will be expressed in all earnest desire to relate the outward conduct to the inward experience and to the spiritual attitude of the heart.

Humility. The Christian must live a life of humility toward God and Mankind and never exalt himself above others. Paul made a pertinent remark concerning humility when he exhorted every person "not to think of himself more highly than he ought to think." He commanded: "Be ye kindly affectioned one to another with brotherly love in honor preferring one another." Paul believed that the Christian should humbly consider another's welfare before personal desires. (Romans 12: 3, 10)

Pride is the parent of gross sins and the spirit of pride causes bitter factions in the body of believers. The Christian must be conscious that believers are a mere recipient of the grace of God and that all stand equal before God. The believer must never take pride in personal knowledge or strength, because the sufficiency for the Christian life is always in God. (2 Corinthians 3:5)

Faithfulness. The Christian owes it to fellow believers to be faithful. A believer must stand steadfast and unmovable in the faith and be firm in a stand for the truth and uphold the New Testament standard of conduct with all diligence. This steadfastness will give life a balance and will gender confidence. (1 Corinthians 15:58)

Spiritual Growth. The believer must not only stand firm and defend the faith, but must grow and mature and enjoy spiritual progress. Each believer is obligated to the brotherhood to "grow in grace and knowledge." (2 Peter 2:18; Colossians 1:9-11)

Kindness.   There must be a friendly atmosphere of good will present in the brotherhood. The Christian must have the welfare of all believers at heart. There should never be any bitterness or ill will permitted among the believers. Note these words in Ephesians: "Let all bitterness, and wrath, and anger, and clamor, and evil speaking, be put away from you, with all malice: And be ye kind one to another, tenderhearted, forgiving one another, even as God for Christ's sake hath forgiven you." (Ephesians 4:31, 32; 2 Corinthians2:7, 8)

The inner nature of the Christian life is such that the believer desires and works for the spiritual and material welfare of the brotherhood.

Outward Manifestations of the Life. The life of love among believers will express itself in Christian conduct that reveals its inner character. The fellowship will be an "active love" that manifests itself in word and deed.   All conduct will be "rooted and grounded in love." (Ephesians 3:16-21)

Within the group life of the church, the Holy Spirit constantly brings every member to confront the absolute holiness of Jesus Christ. All must walk with a contrite heart, accepting forgiveness from the same God whose holiness judges them. Certain standards of discipleship are agreed upon with the brotherhood, and no member passes private judgmental opinion upon another. The entire body of believers seeks to maintain purity of faith, holiness of life, and unity of fellowship by redemptive discipline.

To accomplish this, each believer must "walk in love" and avoid everything that could be harmful to others. The believer should always speak "the truth in love" and express the truth in all of life's activities among the brotherhood. In an effort to maintain order and mutual understanding, the Christian ought to bear with others and make allowance for their actions. By love, the believers should "serve one another." An active concern for the spiritual welfare of the believers must be demonstrated. The agreement in the brotherhood must always be: "let us therefore follow after the things which make for peace and the things wherewith one may edify another." Spiritual care for the brotherhood is only part of brotherly love. It is also expressed in mutual co-operation and helpfulness in all of life.

An Example in Life and Service

When a member of the brotherhood breaks ranks with un-Christian conduct, the entire group suffers and mourns. The erring one is made aware of conditions by the spiritual example of the Fellowship. They are called, with compassion, to repent and to reunite their life with the living fellowship. With love and tenderness, those who are spiritual lead the erring one back to an active fellowship with God and his fellow beings. (Ephesians 4:2, 15; Galatians 5:13; Romans 14:19)

The Christian fellowship carries with it certain responsibilities. Decisions about conduct must be made

not only in the light of the believer's relationship to God, but also in regard to relationship to the brotherhood. Christians should always remember that others are watching their example. One may have to forego something considered harmless for the sake of a Christian example. The believer's reason for abstaining from various "questionable" activities does not rest upon a legalistic argument, but rather such abstinence is dependent upon the love for Jesus and concern for the
conscience of a weaker believer.

There are many areas of life where a mature Christian may not see basic harm; however, participation in such areas may cause a weaker person to stumble. Christians must be careful not to offend those who follow their example. A good illustration of this situation can be found in Paul's first letter to the Corinthians 8:1. To the Corinthian saints who trusted in the true God, the many idols of the city and the consequent sacrifices meant nothing. Some felt that since they did not recognize the idol gods that it would be permissible to eat the meat sold in the market that had been dedicated to the idols. However, Paul seemed to say that the stronger Christian must not eat the meat because a weaker person would not fully understand the whole matter. A believer should never become a stumbling block to those in the brotherhood who are weak (vulnerable, immature).

No individual believer can come to the fullness of the statue of Christ by himself. It takes the whole Christian brotherhood working together to achieve such perfection. However, each believer must make a contribution to the edifying of the brotherhood. The contribution can best be made by living a life of love and by being an example in service. The believer must ask whether or not their Christian example challenges others to live more consecrated lives and if the way in which the Christian faith is maintained is a good example for other believers.

XVI. DUTY TO ONE'S NEIGHBOR

A proper attitude toward those outside the Christian fellowship must also be maintained. The idea of universal benevolence is clearly expressed in Galatians: "As we have therefore opportunity, let us do good unto all men, especially unto them who are of the household of faith." Paul said; "Follow that which is good, both among yourselves and to all men." The Christian must manifest a spirit of forbearance and kindness toward all people, because the coming of Christ is near. The believer must always seek the best interest of one's neighbor. (Galatians 6:10; 1 Thessalonians 9:15; Philippians 4:5)

Christian love is a strong force in one's social life and should have first place on any list of social virtues. "Love worketh no ill to his neighbor; therefore love is the fulfilling of the law." Concerning the virtues of faith, hope, and love, Paul stated: "The greatest of these is love." The life of love manifested toward other believers will also be evident in the Christian's relations with all people. He is commanded to love the neighbor with the same love as for himself and the brotherhood. This is a vital part of the believer's Christian witness. (Romans 13:10; 1 Corinthians 13:13)

The meaning of "neighbor" has been much discussed. In Leviticus the term is used to regulate the relations within the nation of Israel. The Old Testament meaning of neighbor was of value in uniting Israel and preventing their exposure to the moral and spiritual evils found outside the covenant. However, the New Testament meaning of "neighbor" is much wider. It is evident that Jesus, in His teaching concerning the neighbor, referred to more than just personal friends, relatives, or fellow citizens. He included even the enemy.

One of the greatest commands of all time is this: "Thou shalt love thy neighbor as thyself." (Matthew 23:39) The duty to one's neighbor is closely related to the individual's duty to himself. (See XII. DUTY TO SELF) An individual must first consider personal concerns. This is a basic requirement of the plan of God. When this obligation to self and to God is fulfilled, the individual will not neglect the responsibility as a Christian neighbor.

The parable of the Good Samaritan teaches that every person in need is a neighbor regardless of race, station, or creed, and that every person who aids another displays the neighborly spirit. Not only are those who live next door, or in the same community considered to be the Christian's neighbor, but anyone in the world in any kind of need is a neighbor. The needy person does not have to belong to the believer's church, be a citizen of the same country, or of the same race to be considered a neighbor. A basic need is the only requirement. Even unbelievers are neighbors of the Christian community, and each individual believer has a spiritual obligation to them.

Such as the Christian possesses, mentally, physically, and socially, must be shared with those in need. By doing so, one is just being a good neighbor. (Luke 10:25-37)

XVII. DUTY TO ONE'S ENEMY

The Christian must believe that love is stronger than an enemy they may have and must never compromise obedience to Christ's command: "Love your enemies." (Matthew 5:43, 44) The believer must decide once and for all that discipleship means absolute obedience to Christ. A comfortable retreat back to Old Testament ethics is not acceptable, because it is something less than the redeeming Christian love for the enemy.

"Love your enemies" is not a counsel of perfection for selected saints, it is a general law of the Kingdom; it is a precept of that exceeding righteousness that Jesus requires of all who follow Him. The law of retaliation was replaced by Jesus. He is the example. Jesus taught nonresistance by precept and by example. However, His application of this truth was personal and did not include the defense of others. A believer can defend the faith, protect the family, and life, but must never retaliate or seek revenge for personal reasons.

Can one love an enemy and do good to them that despitefully use or abuse? Many persons regard this as an extremely difficult duty, and others think it is impossible. Certainly it is unnatural to love an enemy, because to do so is spiritual work. Yet, the believer is commanded to love all enemies. It is the spirit of Christ who prayed;

"Father, forgive them, for they know not what they do" that motivates such love. An understanding that it is not the person but sin that causes wrong conduct creates a desire to pray earnestly that the enemy will be delivered from the ways of sin and will be brought into fellowship with God and Man. (Luke 23:34; Romans 7:29)

Patient and calm endurance of the wrongdoer is a Christian characteristic. Christian love is demonstrated by loving the un-loveable. However, loving an enemy does not mean that the wrong is condoned or that the evil conduct is approved. The Christian regards the enemy with compassion, and sympathy and is willing to forgive in an effort to win the person to Christ. Indeed, life is too short to permit any part of any day to be spent in holding a grudge, seeking revenge, or showing an evil spirit. Such a situation always depresses the mind and robs life of its joys, while a forgiving spirit gives joy, peace, and a satisfaction to all of life. It should be remembered that meekness is not weakness. A kind and gracious spirit toward all people is entirely consistent with constructive living. Treating others as Jesus treated them is not a demonstration of weakness, but it is a manifestation of the meekness and tenderness of Christ.

Loving one's enemies is another instance where Christian righteousness is to exceed that of the scribes and the Pharisees. The Christian must maintain a positive, helpful, and prayerful attitude to fulfill the obligation to an enemy.

Positive. The Christian must have a positive attitude toward all enemies. There must be more than just patience.

Loving an enemy is not to forbid oneself a wrong course of action, but to make it a positive duty. The believer must seek ways to express Christian love to all enemies.

Helpful. An attitude of helpfulness will logically follow a positive desire to love. Love must be expressed or it dies. It must flow out in deeds and works of kindness. Mere negative nonresistance is not sufficient. This is clearly stated in Romans:

Recompense to no man evil for evil Provide things honest in the sight of all men. If it be possible, as much as lieth in you, live peaceably with all men. Dearly beloved, avenge not yourselves, but rather give place unto [God's] wrath:... for in so doing thou shalt heap coals of fire on his head. Be not overcome of evil, but overcome evil with good. (Romans 12:17-21)

Evil must be overcome by positive action and by good works humbly done. The enemy is conquered when Christian love destroys the hostility and proves the Christian to be a friend.

Prayerful. Patience or nonresistance is supported by love, and love is sustained by prayer. Loving an enemy can be effective and can be sustained by sincerely praying for the enemy. When a Christian is wrongly used or a personal relationship has been strained because of ill will, the believer must pray for God to change the heart of the evildoer. In the meantime, the Christian must continue to demonstrate the positive virtues of love, mercy, and forgiveness as taught by Jesus.

It is true that the enemy is not justified in mistreating the believer, but the evil doer will have to give account to God. The Christian duty is to love, to pray for, and to deal honestly and justly with all regardless of their action or personal attitude toward the Christian. However, there are some people with whom it seems impossible to get along for any period of time. Paul's counsel should be remembered; "If it be possible, as much as lieth in you, live peaceably with all men. In such cases, after all efforts to effect a change in the enemy's attitude and life have failed, he should be left alone. " (2 Thessalonians 5:14, 15)

The Christian must be certain that this "leaving the enemy alone" is not the result of personal indifference. Such an enemy should head the believer's "prayer list." An enemy that is not changed by prayer and love must still be loved and dealt with justly. Justice is not inconsistent with love, but rather it gives strength and dignity to it. There is no exception—the disciple of Jesus must love even the enemy.

XVIII. DUTY TO THE STATE

What is required of a disciple of Jesus Christ in personal relations with civil government? Through the years, believers of the Christian faith have faced the problems of life and have arrived at certain conclusions concerning the believer's obligation in all areas of life. In the realm of the state, the basic attitude seems to be that each believer should develop a Christian conscience and be determined to apply the Christian way of life to citizenship. (Romans 13:1, 2)

Christianity does not release the believer from the necessity of obedience to civil government. The believer lives under the protection of the state, and is subject to all the ordinances that exist for the furtherance of social harmony and orderly living. This is to be done "for the Lord's sake." The believer has an obligation to pray for the leaders of the state that they might be saved. The Christian and the state have no great difficulty unless the laws of the state violate the Christian's conscience. (1 Peter 2:13-17; 1 Timothy 2:1-4)

Christian Conscience

A Christian conscience is acquired by sharing the fellowship and the activities of Christian people and developing a deep concern for Christian ideals. A Christian conscience, as one's social conscience, can be educated; therefore, the Christian is obligated to cultivate an awareness of the ideals and to make an application of these ideals to individual conduct and personal attitude toward the state. The Christian must assume definite responsibility for maintaining Christian ideals within the state. In this age when public policy is determined by popular opinion, the importance of a Christian social conscience is obvious.

The Christian ought not only to be concerned with the subject of Church and State, but must be vitally concerned with the everyday issues that affect freedom and a decent way of life. It should be noted that believers ought to be concerned also with the construct of God and State. The American Constitution may not permit the state to advance any particular religion or sectarian cause, but the Constitution does not prohibit God being involved in the affairs of state. This is the real issue. Believers must consciously advance the motto: "IN GOD WE TRUST."

What if conscience and the state conflict? The Christian must stand with the people who are closest to the moral ideal and be willing to pay the price for this stand. Peter and John were good examples of the proper attitude: "Whether it be right in the sight of God to hearken unto you more than unto God, judge ye. For we cannot but speak the things which we have seen and heard." (Acts 4:19, 20) The position of believers in a conflict of conscience must be that God is the source of final authority: not the state. This means that believers cannot support each and every position taken by the government. At times it becomes a choice of the lesser of two evils, but it is a choice. Party and personality should not be the determining factor of support for a particular position, but the Christian conscience must rule and reign at the ballot box and in the public arena. When believers are integrated or unified around the love of God their action becomes clear and courageous.

Christian Citizenship

The democratic way of life has a definite relation to the Christian faith. It has been called an off-shoot of the Christian movement. The Christian has an obligation to maintain this way of life and to apply moral principles to public affairs. The Christian has a responsibility to participate in the orderly affairs of the state. The believer must always be Christian in this participation and will be held accountable for personal action or for indifference. Believers can never stop with the normal standard of civic responsibility, but is responsible for maintaining a life on the highest level. The moral and ethical standard of living must be evident in all Christian activity. The believer's warm personality, sincere and inherent love of people, should be coupled with the desire to serve in a Christian application of citizenship responsibility. There must be courage to express Christian convictions and a quality of firmness to stand by decisions believed to be right and just.

The Christian citizen should never evade personal obligations to the government that protects the family and which provides a land of peace in which to live and to worship according to a free conscience. All citizens must equally share the burdens of maintaining a state worthy of God's blessings. The words of Jesus are clear: "Render therefore unto Caesar the things which are Caesar's; and unto God the things that are God's." (Matthew 22:21) Issac Watts expressed it well centuries ago in a hymn:

Let Caesar's due be ever paid;
To Caesar and his throne;
But consciences and souls were made
To be the Lord's alone.

XIX. DUTY TO THE WORLD

The grace of God that brought salvation taught mankind to deny ungodliness and worldly desires and to live soberly, righteously, and godly, in this present world. It is obvious that the Christian is a citizen of two worlds. Jesus prayed: *"I pray not that thou shouldest take them out of the world, but that thou shouldest keep them from the evil."* The Christian must live in God's created world and sustain life by the material thing, but it is clear that the Christian is also a citizen of heaven. (Titus 2:11, 12; John 17:14-16)

The Created World of God

The world belongs to God, its Creator. Satan is called "the god of this world," but Satan has limited power. Although Satan has control of much of the human and material things in the world, Satan is not the creator or ruler of the world. Man is a part of the created world of God. The fact that a man believes in Jesus Christ and trusts Him for salvation does not change this fact. Believes are "in the world," but they are not "of the world." Paul said that "all things" including "the world," belong to those who have learned the truth of God and glory in Jesus Christ. (1 Corinthians 3:21, 22)

The created world is not of itself unclean. Sin is a personal matter and does not reside in things. The world is evil only as a fallen world. The world is under the "curse of sin," but this is directly related to the sin of the human race. "The earth is the Lord's and the fullness thereof." All that God has made is good and may be used to sustain life and to provide joy for the Creation. (Romans 14:14; Psalms 24:1; 35:5)

The Material World of Man

The material world of things may be hostile to the Christian way of life. The world has become a symbol of Man's separation from God and the flesh stands as a symbol of the unredeemed soul. These are destined for destruction by the judgment of God. The attitude of the Christian to the world must be one of extreme caution. Christians must resolutely separate themselves from everything that would defile the soul or the spirit. The fight against this world is not entirely, or even primarily, an external matter; it is a struggle within the very soul of a person. Notice these words of John:

Love not the world, neither the things that are in the world. If any man love the world, the love of the Father is not in him. For all that is in the world, the lust of the flesh, and the lust of the eyes, and the pride of life, is not of the Father, but is of the world. And the world passeth away, and the lust thereof; but he that doeth the will of God abideth forever. (1 John 2: 15-17)

The world that man must not love is "this world." It will pass away. The Christian really belongs to the eternal kingdom of God built on the Word. Believers are at liberty to make use of the material world as God's gifs and to enjoy the created world of God, but these things must always be secondary and passing.

Christians are to use the material world for the advancement of the Kingdom. The material possessions are to be recognized as gifts of God. (2 Corinthians 9:6, 7) The fact that each believer is to give to God's cause "as he hath prospered" is evidence that God is not opposed to prosperity, provided it is used for the advancement of the Kingdom. Believers are to work in the world to provide for their household and the less fortunate. (1 Thessalonians

4:10-12; 2 Thessalonians 3:8-13) The material world must never become the center of existence. It may be used and even enjoyed, but it must always remain secondary to the believer's devotion and concern for the Kingdom.

The Christian should enjoy life and living, but should cultivate an attitude of detachment from the world and maintain personal dependence on Jesus Christ. This world is not home for the Christian; the believer is just passing through. The believer's citizenship is in heaven with all the redeemed. It will be a wonderful time in glory when believers are finally freed from the tug of this world's gravity and can enjoy the freedom and fullness of God's blessings!

XX. DUTY TO THE UNBELIEVER

Discipleship speaks of separation from old ties and an exclusive adherence to Jesus Christ. The line has been clearly drawn between the old and the new life, between the saint and the unbeliever. This raises the question of the relationship between the Christian and the unbeliever.

A basic desire of believers who have experienced the joy of a genuine spiritual consecration is to persuade others to enter into the same experience. This is a spiritual expression of the natural impulse to share any enjoyable experience with others. The primary purpose of the believer's consecration is found in an attitude toward the unbeliever. The compelling missionary attitude of believers is expressed in these words of an unknown poet:

> Can we whose souls are lighted
> With wisdom from on high;
> Can we to souls benighted
> The lamp of life deny?

Christians must be a "light to the lost" and point others to the Savior. The church that practices love will be best able to evangelize. Converts will be attracted to the Christian faith when believers "walk in wisdom toward them that are without." Each individual believer must keep personally pure and "void of offense" if the evangelistic outreach of the church is to be effective.

A Christian tends to reject those who deviate from an accepted standard of living. The more consecrated the believer and the deeper the convictions concerning holiness of heart and life, the more vigorous the rejection. Christians who are committed to Christ and take the accepted standard of discipleship seriously must be aware of this tendency to reject. Discipleship does not afford the believer a point of advantage from which to attack others; the believer must come to the unbeliever with an unconditional offer of Christian love, understanding, and fellowship.

The Christian life is more than merely believing. The believer must live Christ before all associates as a winning witness of grace. A moral life is the whole and Christian living the part. This life is one of grace. All Man stands equal before God: saved by grace though faith. It is easily understood that one will react differently to others when the main purpose for living among them is to honor Jesus Christ and to win them by His love.

Being a believer does not endow one with standards of judgment or special rights and privileges above others. Rather, it obligates the believer to others in a unique way. How easy it would be for the Christian to adopt a superior attitude and to pass unqualified condemnation on the rest of the world. This is why Jesus made it so clear that such misunderstandings would imperil discipleship. Christians are not to judge others. If they do, they will b judged by God as hypocrites themselves, and will jeopardize their Christian fellowship. (Matthew 7:1-12)

Judging others blinds the believer to personal needs. When a believer makes judgments, a new set of standards of good and bad are imposed.

The standard of holiness is to be applied to believers and not to an unbeliever. The holiness of God and the Christian example of believers will condemn and judge the unbeliever. A unbeliever will actually judge himself when brought face to face with a consecrated believer. The source of good is God and exists only as the believer is related to God; therefore, the believer can never use personal goodness as a standard by which to judge others.

As a disciple of Christ, the believer has a new standard of conduct. This standard, however, is the result of a relationship with Christ and not the cause of this relationship; therefore, the believer has no right to judge the unbeliever by the Christian standard of living. The true believer does not see personal righteousness, but sees the righteousness of Jesus and constantly makes personal evaluation by this standard. The Christian seeks to bring unbeliever friends, by precept and example, into a saving knowledge of Jesus Christ, knowing that this is the only way to cause conduct to conform to Christian standards.

Certainly there is a great gulf fixed between the believer and unbelievers, but it is well for the saint to remember that Jesus was a friend of unbelievers. There can be no true partnership, harmony, or agreement between the believer and the unbeliever, because they have nothing in common. (2 Corinthians 6:14-18) Consequently, the believer, being an unbeliever saved by grace, can well understand the unbeliever's state of affairs and assist in finding relief from the burden of sin. It is not a standard of right living that separates the Christian and the unbeliever; it is Christ who stands between them.

The believer must meet the unbeliever as a prospect for the Kingdom. The good news of the gospel should never be forced upon an unwilling heart, but the believer has an obligation to the unbeliever to demonstrate the reality of the Christian experience and to encourage them to seek God. Of course, this can only be done provided the Holy Spirit is drawing the unbeliever toward Christ. The Christian should follow Paul's "all things to all men" example in an effort to save those who will accept Christ and follow Him.

The unbeliever should not be viewed with detachment, because Jesus died for all and the unbeliever has a claim on God's love. Believers ought to seek to make disciples of all unbelieving friends and fervently intercede for the unbeliever's salvation. The unbeliever should be encouraged to seek forgiveness, and follow the simple steps to salvation. By loving unconditionally, the believer may effect a condemnation of sin. Once the unbeliever is aware of the Spirit's tug and understands the steps to salvation, the believer can lead this person into a saving knowledge of Jesus. The true disciple does not have any special privilege or power personally in this relationship with the unbeliever. The relationship is regulated by the Holy Spirit and the believer's concern for the unbeliever. A simple rule of thumb that Jesus gave the disciples is clear: "All things whatsoever ye would that men should do to you, do ye even so to them." (Matthew 7:12) When this simple rule is followed, the Christian forfeits all advantage over others and seeks to bring all unbelievers into fellowship with God.

Study and Review Questions for Section Four

1. What is Man's primary duty?
2. What are the logical consequences of recognizing God as the Eternal Father?
3. Why was "duty to self" place second in this section?
4. Discuss the believer's self-development. Why the order: mental, physical, spiritual, and social?
5. What is the role of the church in Christian marriage?
6. Discuss the problems involved in marriage when only one is a believer. Apply the triangle relationship to this situation.
7. How are the church and the home related? How can they cooperate for mutual benefit?
8. Why should believers join a local church?
9. What are the believer's obligations to the church?
10. How can church membership be kept meaningful?
11. Discuss the church as a fellowship?
12. What are the characteristics expressed in a life of love toward the brotherhood?
13. Discuss the meaning of neighbor.
14. What attitudes must the Christian maintain to fulfill the obligation of love for an enemy?
15. What should be the believer's basic attitude toward the state?
16. What must the Christian do if conscience and the state conflict?
17. Why should the Christian cultivate a detachment from the material community?
18. Discuss the believer's final freedom from the tug of this world.
19. Should Christians judge others? What are the results of judging others?
20. Discuss the tendency to reject people who deviate from your standard of living.

BIBLIOGRAPHY

The original bibliography is listed below. The books are out of print now, but these are the authors that influenced the original text (1962). Present readers can go to Books in Print and find at least 100 books available on many aspects of Discipleship.

Barnette, Henlee H., *Introducing Christian Ethics.* Nashville: Broadman Press, 1961

Bornkamm, Gunther, *Jesus of Nazareth.* New York: Harper and Brothers, translation of the 1959 edition.

Cochran, Leonard H., *Man at His Best.* New York: Abingdon Press, 1957.

Cook, Robert A., *Steps to Maturity.* Wheaton: Scripture Press Foundation, 1960.

Copi, Irving M., *Introduction to Logic.* New York: The MacMillian Company, 1953.

Eavy, C. B., *Principles of Christian Ethics.* Grand Rapids: Zondervan Publishing House, 1958.

Ellwood, Charles A., *The World's Need of Christ.* New York: Abingdon-Cokesbury, 1940.

Harrison, Everett F., Geoffrey W. Bromomite, and Carl F. H. Henry, *Baker's Dictionary of Theology.* Grand Rapids: Baker Book House, 1960.

Keyser, Leander S., *A System of General Ethics.* Burlington, Iowa: The Luthern Literary Board, 1954.

King, Geoffrey R., *Truth for Our Time.* Grand Rapids: Wm. B. Eerdmans Publishing Company, 1957.

Knudson, Albert C., *The Principles of Christian Ethics.* New York: Abingdon-Cokesbury Press, 1943.

Maston, T. B., *The Christian in the Modern World.* Nashville: Convention Press, 1952.

Meyer, F. B., *The Sermon on the Mount.* Grand Rapids: Baker Book House, 1959.

Miller, Paul M., *Group Dynamics in Evangelism.* Scottdale,
  Pennsylvania: Herald Press, 1958.

Oldham, J. H., *Life is Commitment.* New York: Association
  Press, 1959, abridgement edition.

Oldham, Dale, *Living Close to God.* Anderson, Indiana: The
  Warner Press, 1957.

Spence, H. D. M. and Joseph S. Exell, *The Pulpit Commentary.*
  Grand Rapids: Wm. E. Eerdmans Publishing Company,
  1950.

Spike, Robert W., *Tests of a Living Church.* New York:
  Association Press, 1961.

Stevenson, Herbert F. (ed.), *Keswick's Authentic Voice.* Grand
  Rapids: Zondervan Publishing House, 1959.

Tenny, Merrill C., *New Testament Survey.* Grand Rapids:
  Wm. B. Eerdmans Publishing Company, 1960.

White, Reginald E. O., *The Stranger of Galilee.* Grand Rapids:
  Wm. B. Eerdmans Publishing Company, 1960.

Yates, J. Clyde, *Our Marching Orders in Evangelism.* New
  York: The American Press, 1957.

Other Books by Author

Books by Hollis L. Green, ThD, PhD

[   ] Why Churches Die
[   ] Sympathetic Leadership Cybernetics
[   ] Why Christianity Fails in America
[   ] SO TALES - Volume One
[   ] Philosophy of Adult Education
[   ] SO TALES Volume Two
[   ] DISCIPLESHIP
[   ] Why Wait Till Sunday?
[   ] Integrating Moral Values
[   ] Understanding Scientific Research
[   ] Interpreting an Author's Words
[   ] Titanic Lessons
[   ] Things Learned and Passed to my Sons
[   ] SLEEPY TOWN Lullaby and Story
[   ] Fighting the Amalekites
[   ] Love's Conversation
[   ] SO TALES Volume Three
[   ] Understanding Graduate Research
[   ] Lessons from Luke – NT 101
[   ] All Believers are Created Equal
[   ] Growing a New Testament Church
[   ] How to Build a Better Spouse Trap
[   ] Where in the World are you Going?
[   ] Hitching your Star to a Wagon
[   ] Climbing the Heights
[   ] A Composite New Testament Man

Order from:

GlobalEdAdvancePress
345 Barton Road at Lone Mountain, Dayton, TN 37321-7635 USA
GlobalEdAdvance@aol.com

GlobalEdAdvance Press
Tennessee 37321-7635
ISBN 978-9796019-5-8